THE MURDERER HUNTERS

This edition first published in Great Britain in 2006
By André Deutsch Limited
20 Mortimer Street
London W1T 3JW

First published as *Murder Trail* by Granada Media, 2002

Text copyright © Colin Bell 2002
Programme concept and materials © copyright Granada Media Group 2002

Murder Trail is a Granada Bristol production for Channel Five (UK)
and The Learning Channel (US)

The right of Colin Bell to be identified as the author of this work has
been asserted by him in accordance with the Copyright, Designs and
Patents Act 1988

A catalogue record is available from the British Library

ISBN 0-23300-161-1

The publishers and the tv production team would like to thank the Police
Departments and in all eight cases for their help
and co-operation. We would like to thank the following for their help

Hillside Stra   er Boren, Los Angeles Court of Appeal
Aileen Wuorn   s – Mercy Stephens, Florida Department Law Enforcement;
        Kelley, Volusia County Sheriff's Office

Every effort has been made to acknowledge correctly the source and/or
copyright holder of each picture, and Granada Media apologises for
any unintentional errors or omissions which will be corrected in future
editions of this book.

Typeset by E-Type, Liverpool

Printed and bound in Great Britain

2 4 6 8 10 9 7 5 3

THE MURDERER HUNTERS

THE DETECTIVES' INSIDE STORIES

Colin Bell

André Deutsch

CONTENTS

INTRODUCTION

The crimes and criminals covered in both the television series and this book raise a number of disquieting thoughts, and not just because they are all singularly brutal. For a start, only one – the murder of their parents by the Menendez Brothers – seems to have the kind of rational motive we, and traditional detectives in both fact and fiction, expect. For all the grotesque allegations made in their defence, it seems fairly clear that Erik and Lyle Menendez wanted to eliminate all possible risk that their parents' $14 million might not be theirs to do with as they wished, and sooner rather than later.

Callous as that murder was, it is also the only one dealt with which conforms to the normal rule – victims are, in the vast majority of routine homicides, killed by someone they know. Relatives, lovers, rivals, drinking partners, fellow criminals. All experienced police officers look first for a motive, and a perpetrator, closely connected to the personal life of the victim.

But in seven out of these eight cases, no such connection could normally be made. The law enforcement agencies were confronted with multiple killings of strangers by a stranger, the general public and the media by the nightmare thought that anybody, however innocent, might be chosen at random by a murderer or murderers simply because the urge to kill had come upon them.

Certainly, in several cases, the killings were accompanied by thefts – but not planned and targeted on those with something valuable to steal, merely opportunistic thefts of whatever caught the killer's eye after having first chosen someone to kill. Indeed, although Richard Ramirez was a burglar, his haul from his murder victims was trivial, and, as with the others discussed here, seems often to have represented a form of grisly trophy-hunting rather than professional larceny.

In at least three cases, those of David Carpenter, Bobby Joe Long and the Hillside Stranglers, there is more than a suspicion that the murderer went equipped to take a photographic record of his crime, producing even more satisfying trophies than a few scraps of jewellery or clothing.

Most chilling of all, although six of these cases involve multiple sexual assaults, they lend powerful backing to the argument that rape isn't about sex at all – it is simply another expression of tyrannical power over another human being. Testosterone is unquestionably a dangerous drug, but there is a case for saying that it may have played a bigger part in the deaths of those men who foolishly gave lifts to Aileen Wuornos, than in the deaths of the women killed by Buono, Bianchi, Milat, Carpenter and Ramirez. They raped, they sodomized – but above all, they exercised a supreme satanic power over their helpless victims. Bobby Joe Long, of course, ran two entirely distinct criminal careers – one as a rapist who stole but did not kill, and one as a killer who also raped. While David Berkowitz simply killed.

One further theory which investigating officers entertained in several of these cases (Milat, Buono, Long, perhaps Carpenter) is that killing was necessary to break the ultimate taboo: necrophilia. There is evidence that both Buono and Long raped *during* the process of killing, but the condition in which most victims were discovered precluded any certainties at autopsy.

There is compelling evidence in several of these cases that, whatever the original motive may have been, perhaps simply the lust for power, expressed in sexual assault, and an awareness that dead witnesses cannot testify, during the course of the killer's development, the real addiction came to be the killing itself. For instance, while David Berkowitz and Aileen Wuornos stuck with their signature hand-guns, others experimented with ever-more obscene and terrifying methods – not just guns, knives and clubs, but machetes, ceremonial swords, lethal injection, and electrocution. For those whose lives had been dogged by failure, and that covers quite a few of these killers (and many of their victims), forcing another human being to strip, to be bound, to be beaten, raped, tortured, and then killed in peculiarly horrible ways was the ultimate gratification.

Serial killing is not, of course, new – Vlad the Impaler, Sawney Bean, Sweeney Todd, Bluebeard and others have floated from fact to fiction to nightmare throughout the centuries – but it does appear to have become more common. I say 'appear' for the very good reason that we only know there's a serial killer at large when multiple bodies are actually discovered, and can be linked by detective work and forensic science. Not every killer transports his victims in a car whose distinctive carpet constantly sheds fibre, nor leaves a trail of his virtually unique shoe-prints. The English physician Harold Shipman, whose ultimate tally, at well over 200, far outranks those dealt with here, might very possibly have got clean away if he'd been a little more restrained. Certainly no-one thought to wonder quite why his female patients had such a poor life-expectancy until he had been at work for nearly 20 years. In a number of the cases covered here, experienced investigators are convinced that other victims were never discovered, or perhaps discovered but not linked. When, like Ivan Milat, Bobby Joe Long or David Carpenter, you have thousands of acres of wilderness at your disposal, and the depredations of climate and animal life to assist the cover-up, it must be possible.

Of course, even when the investigating officers all accept and agree that they do have a serial killer on their hands, mistakes can be made. In almost every one of these cases, at least one informant or clue was ignored, pigeon-holed, mishandled. But that's not uncommon. In Britain, both Peter Sutcliffe and Robert Black eluded 'Task Forces' of high-profile policemen for years. And, as Gary Terry of Hillsborough County, Florida, points out, just because there's a serial killer at work doesn't mean all the other criminals take a vacation. No matter what the public outcry (and the news media everywhere nowadays ferment panic, speculation and criticism) no law agency can simply give up on every other crime for the duration. Which is one reason why detectives like Frank Salerno take a jaundiced view of 'Task Forces' in any case – if other police departments are asked to second staff to one, they won't necessarily want to send their very best, because they'll still have other cases of their own to solve.

Hindsight can, of course, make almost any investigation look inept. Because we now know the significance of Kenneth Bianchi's bogus police badge, we are censorious of the police who accepted his denial. Because we now know the importance of the early mentions of suspect names in several of these inquiries, we are appalled that some were scarcely noticed, let alone followed up. But in cases of this sort, where the fragments of information can flood in in their thousands, investigators have no rational choice but to prioritize, and to do so on what they think they know already – even if that means that an early photofit or artist's impression mistakenly gives priority to suspects of the wrong physical type entirely.

In several of these cases, there was a further complication: sheer political and territorial rivalry between investigating agencies. The serial killer in the automobile age can roam wherever they wish, hopping from city to city, out into the rural counties, state to state, killing in one jurisdiction, dumping bodies in another. Information which might be priceless to one agency is meaningless to another, or jealously guarded out of sheer bloody-mindedness. The relationship between the City of Los Angeles Police Department and the Sheriff's Office of Los Angeles County was plainly not made in Heaven, even without the bickering between both and the police forces of the smaller cities in their area.

Most depressing of all, you'll probably share with me the suspicion that some of the monsters whose eventual arrest and conviction are detailed here might well have got away with it if they had maintained their discipline. If Kenneth Bianchi hadn't suddenly turned to murdering two women whom everyone knew he'd arranged to meet; if Bobby Joe Long had not suddenly felt a twinge of compassion for Lisa McVey; if David Carpenter hadn't chosen a workmate, instead of a random visitor to the forest trails, to be a victim; would they, *could* they, still be at large? It's not impossible.

And one final terrifying thought: the FBI has suggested that at any one time, somewhere between 20 and 30 serial murderers are going about their dreadful business up and down the United States. If any of them have spotless school and employment records, have always got on well with their

Mothers and other women, vary their weapons and their vehicles, and scrupulously stick to total strangers for their prey, they may well get away with it.

DAVID BERKOWITZ –
SON OF SAM

Ten months into the investigation, and at the scene of the sixth deadly assault which the New York police had every reason to believe was the work of the same psychotic killer, investigating officers found a letter. It was addressed to their senior officer.

'Dear Captain Joseph Borrelli,
I am deeply hurt by your calling me a wemon hater. I am not. But I am a monster. I am the 'Son of Sam'. I am a little brat.
When Father Sam gets drunk he gets mean. He beats his family. Sometimes he ties me up to the back of the house. Other times he locks me in the garage. Sam loves to drink blood.
'Go out and kill,' commands Father Sam.
Behind our house some rest. Mostly young – raped and slaughtered – their blood drained – just bones now.

Papa Sam keeps me locked in the attic too. I can't get out, but I look out the attic window and watch the world go by.

I feel like an outsider. I am on a different wavelength then everybody else – programmed to kill.

However, to stop me you must kill me. Attention all police: shoot me first – shoot to kill or else keep out of my way or you will die!

Papa Sam is old now. He needs some blood to preserve his youth. He has had too many heart attacks. 'Ugh, me hoot, it hurts, sonny boy.'

I miss my pretty princess most of all. She's resting in our ladies house. But I'll see her soon.

I am the 'Monster' – 'Beelzebub' – the chubby behe-mouth.

I love to hunt. Prowling the streets looking for fair game – tasty meat. The wemon of Queens are prettyist of all. It must be the water they drink. I live for the hunt – my life. Blood for papa.

Mr. Borrelli, sir, I don't want to kill any more. No sur, but I must, 'honour thy father.'

I want to make love to the world. I love people. I don't belong on earth. Return me to yahoos.

To the people of Queens, I love you. And I want to wish all of you a happy Easter. May God bless you in this life and the next.

I say goodbye and goodnight.

Police: let me haunt you with these words; I'll be back! I'll be back!

To be interpreted as – bang bang bang bang, bang – ugh!! Yours in murder,

Mr. Monster.'

Given where it had been found – next to the bodies of Valentina Suriani and her boyfriend Alexander Esau in their parked car – and that they had been shot by the same gun which had been used in a series of earlier 'lovers' lane' murders, Captain Borrelli didn't doubt that it came from the unknown serial killer. But although the press, and the police, now had a label for the case – 'Son of Sam' – they didn't have much more. The letter and its envelope had been so frequently and carelessly handled that it carried a wide and confusing variety of fingerprints.

But of course, it did offer certain other hints – nothing so strong as a clue, but grounds for informed hypothesis. For a start, nobody was going to believe that a person who found no difficulty with 'wavelength', 'programmed' or 'Beelzebub' would genuinely misspell 'women'.

And by this stage, just about anything was worth exploring: Son of Sam had got the entire city of New York, and more especially, the boroughs of the Bronx, Queens and Brooklyn, terrified. Just to add to the pressure, from the standpoint of the NYPD, it was a Mayoral election year, and the politicians at City Hall, just along from Number One, Police Plaza, were being as big a nuisance as the press.

Now this was April of 1977, but the story really began in the preceding year: in fact, in the very early hours of 29 July 1976, in the Bronx.

New York is one of the world's biggest magnets for tourists, both American and foreign, but it's safe to say that very few of the visitors ever venture beyond Manhattan, save perhaps to take the ferry to Staten Island. The other three boroughs of the city may be home to the great majority of New York's citizens, but they remain *terra incognita* to the world at large. The Bronx is up, as the song says, and gave its name to the American term for a ribald raspberry noise, the 'Bronx cheer': Queens is what the bus or cab taking people to and from JFK airport gets through as quickly as it can: and Brooklyn is what you see across the East River from FDR Drive, sweeping down Manhattan from north to south. So the average visitor might find it difficult to imagine that the New York they know, all densely-packed skyscrapers on the most valuable island in the world, does actually have outlying districts where lovers' lanes can be found.

Son of Sam was to make the city's quieter, darker, more secluded parking places high-risk areas for the best part of a year, but his first killing took place right outside an apartment block. That late July night of 1976, two young women, Donna Lauria and Jody Valenti, were chatting in Jody's car outside the Lauria home, and had already been told by Donna's parents it was time for bed, when Jody recalled Donna suddenly spotting a strange man standing by the car, and wondering who he could be and what he could want.

As she did so, the man pulled out a handgun from a paper bag, stooped, and fired five shots into the parked Oldsmobile. Donna died instantly from a bullet in the neck while Jody, wounded in the leg, leaned on the horn and screamed. Donna's father raced out in his pyjamas – but too late to save his daughter, or catch the fleeing murderer. And Jody's description was inevitably vague.

There seemed to be no clues, nor any obvious motive. The police even toyed with the notion that it may have been a mistaken hit by criminals on the wrong target, but eventually inclined to the view that the killer could only be a psycho. Who that might be, they had no idea.

Son of Sam lay low for several months, until 23 October 1976. That night, there was a farewell party at a bar in Flushing for a young man called Carl Denaro, who was about to join the Air Force. After the party Carl drove a girlfriend, Rosemary Keenan, home, and parked nearby to say his goodbyes. Just as before, the couple suddenly became aware of a strange man peering into their car – who then fired five shots into it.

Carl was hit in the head – but Rosemary, unwounded, though naturally hysterical, nevertheless had the sense to drive the car back to the bar where Carl's friends still were, and they in turn rushed him to hospital. Surgeons were able to save his life, but not his hoped-for career in the Air Force.

Once more, there seemed no real clues or motive – and we can be sure the police made every effort, since Rosemary's father was a detective in the Homicide Division in Queens. But the smallest glimmer of progress was made in the Police Department's laboratory. Although the bullets recovered from the Bronx victims and from Carl were too badly mashed to offer positive proof of any link, their calibre was unusual. As Jim Harran, the then-Commander of the lab, explains: 'I was told there was a match in that .44 calibre bullets had been used in a case up in the Bronx and now in a case in Queen's. That calibre of gun is not common in New York City – I think in the five years prior to that there had only been one case we'd seen. So we notified the Queens homicide squad that there was a strong possibility that these two cases were related.'

Not much to go on, really. But a little over a month later, on the evening of 26 November 1976, two teenage girls, Donna DeMasi and Joanne Lomino, had returned from a late-night movie by bus, and begun walking the short distance to Joanne's home in the Floral Park section of Queens, when Joanne saw a man behind them. She urged Donna to walk a little faster, but the man followed them, and then spoke to them as if to ask directions. 'Do you know where...' he said, but instead of continuing, pulled a gun and fired at them.

Both girls were hit, but as they began to scream, the assailant emptied his gun at a nearby house before making off. The noise had been heard by Joanne's parents, who burst out of their house and immediately rushed the girls to hospital. Donna, it turned out, had been lucky – a bullet had passed within a quarter of an inch of her spine before exiting: Joanne had not – her bullet had shattered her spine, leaving her paraplegic.

By now the police at least were beginning to refer to 'The .44 Calibre Killer' and to suspect that they were looking for a psycho, but they had no idea where they should be looking.

Indeed, in retrospect, some of those involved now concede that if Son of Sam hadn't stuck to his .44, they might never have linked the separate incidents together at all, even as a hypothesis. Jim Harran spells it out: 'If it wasn't for the fact that he was using the .44 calibre gun, it would not have been recognized that we had a serial killer.'

The killer took another break over the long holiday period from Thanksgiving through Christmas and New Year, while the police wondered what they might possibly do to track down an anonymous murderer, or stop him striking again. Unfortunately, there was nothing – and around midnight on 30 January 1977, strike he did.

Christine Freund and her fiancé John Diel left the Wine Gallery in Queens and got into John's car. Neither noticed the man who had watched them as they did so, and approached the parked car as they sat. Two shots exploded the windscreen, both hitting Christine, who survived only long enough to reach the hospital. Neighbours who had heard the shots had called the police, but the investigating officers still did not jump to the immediate conclusion that this was the serial killer. In fact, they began by exploring the possibility that it was someone who had a personal quarrel with Christine, an avenue which quickly petered out.

More significantly, one of the first detectives at the scene, Marlon Hopkins, who had been surprised to hear that a homicide had taken place in Forest Hills – 'a very affluent, low-crime area' as he remembers – found a bullet on the dashboard of the car. A distinctive bullet, which he turned in to his immediate superior, Detective Sergeant Joe Coffey, who spotted that an unusual calibre weapon had been used, and checked around the city's other divisions for any previous incidents involving a .44. As soon as he did so, the pattern began to fall into place. Not just the same type of weapon, but a very similar type of MO – *modus operandi*, the Latin term which policemen almost everywhere use to categorize an offender's distinctive style of behaviour.

By this time, it had become clear that something more cohesive than a series of separate investigations by individual detectives in scattered precincts from the Bronx to Queens was needed. And Coffey's boss, Captain Joe Borrelli of Homicide in Queens, was appointed to head a special Task Force, whose focus was quickly sharpened by the news from the NYPD ballistics experts that the gun – still the only real clue – had been narrowed down to a .44 Bulldog, made by Charter Arms of Connecticut.

No rational motive, no particular suspect, no confident and dependable witness – but, at least, a gun. Bob Freglio was employed at the time as a specialist ballistics detective with the NYPD, a job which, as he says, meant 'going to the various morgues in the city to recover any bullets. The bullets would then be brought back to our office, catalogued, weighed, examined, checked for rifling marks and placed in a file which is specific for calibre. Now, when the first .44 calibre bullet or bullets came in at the first shooting, it's quite an unusual calibre. We didn't get many .44s. When the second came in, now you start putting two and two together, and it's very unusual, though it happened in different areas. When the third shooting occurred, everybody is up in arms, because this is like a serial killer we have.'

Bob and his colleagues methodically checked out everything that those bullets told them, and concluded that the killer's weapon was unquestionably a Bulldog from Charter Arms, a company with nothing like the prominence of Colt or Smith & Wesson, but which had produced this particular model with a specialized market in view – Sky Marshals, who needed a gun which would stop a hi-jacker, but not carry on to penetrate the pressurized skin of an aircraft. Actually, Bob's professional view was that 'it's a cheaply-made gun. I personally wouldn't want to carry one: it's got too much of a recoil, it's a gun that kills when you hit something and it's not a self-defence gun. It's just too heavy to carry.'

The only problem with this first indisputable clue was that, whatever it's quality and characteristics, the Charter Arms Bulldog had already sold to 28,000 customers across America. Doggedly, the new task force under Joe Borelli began circulating the country's 35,000 registered arms dealers for details of their sales.

In the Internet age,that may sound elementary, even easy, but Joe Borelli reminds us that this was still the age of the 3" x 5" filing card. 'Ultimately' he remembers ' we had over ten thousand of those cards.'

Still, there did now seem something, however vague, for the task force (Borelli preferred then, as now, to call it 'an investigative group') to tackle. It can't be said that Borelli was optimistic – on the back of 35 years' experience he says, quite categorically, 'If you're going to solve a homicide, you solve it in the first 24 hours.'

The killer gave them something more to solve. On the evening of Tuesday, 8 March 1977, an undergraduate from Barnard College, one of the most highly-regarded schools in America, was walking home in that same affluent Forest Hills area. Virginia Voskerichian's family had fled Armenia for America at the height of the Cold War, and prospered. Their home on Dartmouth Street, like Virginia's college place, testified to that. But as she walked the last few yards to safety, a man approached her from the opposite direction, drew a gun and pointed it at her face. A single shot passed through the college books she had raised in an instinctive gesture of defence, and killed her.

This time, there was a witness. As he ran away, the killer greeted him. 'Hi, mister', he said.

There might even have been an arrest. A cruising police car spotted a man running in a suspicious manner, and the officers were about to flag him down when they heard on their radio that there had been a shooting on nearby Dartmouth Street. Instead of stopping the fugitive, they wheeled about and rushed to Dartmouth Street.

Although the crime didn't reflect well on the police, it did mark an enormous change in their approach. Possibly because New York Mayor Abe Beame was growing apprehensive about his chances of re-election, possibly because everyone now appreciated that there really was a serial killer on the loose, Joe Borelli's 'investigative group' was dramatically upgraded into 'Operation Omega' – and a higher-ranking officer, Deputy Inspector Timothy Dowd, was put in overall charge. Eventually, something like 300 detectives from all over the city's scattered precincts were to be involved.

To no one's surprise, the bullet which had killed Virginia Voskerichian matched those from the earlier shootings – but the witness could offer nothing anywhere as distinctive about the assumed killer who had greeted him. At the first of what was to prove a regular series of press conferences, the Police Commissioner finally told the people of New York that ballistics had firmly tied in all the shootings to one perpetrator. But he had to say that all they had apart from that was a description of 'a white male, 25 to 30 years old, six feet tall, medium build, with dark hair.' Which, in a city of ten million, wasn't exactly definitive.

Inevitably, the media gave the serial killings extensive coverage. And inevitably, the people of the city began to panic – a mad gunman who seemed to pick attractive young women at random for his victims and want nothing more than to empty his gun into them, without any more commonplace motive was, as one cop later admitted, comparable only to a terrorist.

Despite the appointment of Dowd, Borelli remained the effective leader of the working detectives, and he was prepared to accept any help he could get. According to Harvey Schlossberg, who prepared a psychological profile of the kind of man who would commit such crimes, 'Joe was a professional, so what he did was utilized all the resources he could possibly have. He used street-smart detectives, he used clairvoyants, mystics, anybody that would offer help. He knew that when you have nothing, anything you could gather could be useful, so when he came to me he said, "You know, this is really a difficult case; we don't have much to go on", so perhaps if I could help them narrow down a personality type then he could look through the different leads they were getting – the long range of suspects – and use it to help classify the criminal.'

Schlossberg, on the basis of what little evidence they had, concluded that the killer was attempting to evade detection, trying to confound the police, and got pleasure from leading the police in a kind of cat-and-mouse game. He also concluded that it was indeed a case of a psychopathic personality.

'I arrived at a character that first of all, obviously had problems with women – in one case he selected a male, but that male had long hair and could, in the dark, be taken for a female. He selected places where people would go for privacy, quiet, darkness – so he wanted somewhere where he wouldn't get caught. Since he did have these problems with women, it was very unlikely he'd be married: he'd probably live alone. Since it involved travel, it involved maintaining a vehicle, registering it, paying insurance for it: therefore he must work, and with this personality it would be unlikely for him to work with other people in close contact because he'd be suspicious, paranoid, thinking everybody's plotting against him. And he certainly couldn't work with females, so he would do some kind of isolated job where he handled objects, not people, and so the guess I just made was a kind of job like sorting mail in the Post Office, or sitting in front of a computer.'

Schlossberg was eventually to be proved uncannily accurate. But another offer of outside help didn't really impress Borelli. He recollects sitting in the office one day when the phone rang – 'and there's a Hispanic male voice on the line, and he tells me, "Please don't hang up." He says, "My wife has these abilities, and she's having them now." I can hear this woman speaking in Spanish in the background, and he's translating for me. He says there's going to be another shooting. It's going to be on a street, but it's not a street. It's going to be in the country, but it's not the country. So I was just about to hang up on him, but then he says the car is going to be two-tone, it's going to be dark red and black, and a boy and a girl are going to be killed.' Borelli wrote it all down and mentioned it to colleagues but, frankly, none of them gave it very serious attention – not least because that call came in just before the shooting of Virginia Voskerichian, which didn't match any of the mystic's predictions.

However, Son of Sam's next strike certainly did. On 17 April 1977, two young sweethearts sat necking in their parked car on the service road off the Hutchinson River Parkway in the Bronx. It was a two-tone car, maroon and black. The service road isn't, of course, a street in the normal, urban sense – and it's lined with trees.

At about 3 am another car drew up alongside that of

Valentina Suriani and Alexander Esau. Its driver shot each of them twice, fatally in both cases, and then put a letter into their car – the letter to Borelli, which revealed that the .44 killer styled himself 'Son of Sam.'

Now that letter, as we've seen, didn't offer much direct help – but it certainly fitted Harvey Schlossberg's profile. Here was somebody who wanted to tease the police – not get caught, but enjoy publicity for his cleverness. And the police, perhaps because they didn't want to indulge that vanity, or more probably because they didn't want to provoke any other nuts to chip in their correspondence (just remember how the pursuit of the Yorkshire Ripper was diverted by an entirely bogus claimant) kept the letter quiet.

It was, of course, passed to Jim Harran at the NYPD lab. Although by now a Captain in command of the whole department, Jim was a specialist document examiner. He established that the letter was prepared on loose-leaf paper from a pad, written in pencil, and could at least file all the various finger-prints it had acquired against the possibility of any other document being found. Which is exactly what happened.

At the time, one of New York's best-known newspaper columnists was Jimmy Breslin of the *Long Island News Day*. Long Island is immediately to the East of Manhattan, contains not just Queens and Brooklyn but everything from downmarket East New York to the madly fashionable Hamptons and such oddities as Coney Island and Brighton Beach, and its paper was probably closer to the heart of everyday New York than the better-known New York Times.

Breslin used his column to write an open letter to 'Son of Sam.' It's what columnists do.

He got a reply. After just about everybody on the paper had handled it, they got in touch with the police, and asked if they'd be interested. Jim Harran recalls: 'We sent someone from the laboratory up to *News Day*, got the letter and brought it down for processing. Comparison of the handwriting was relatively straightforward – it was easy to see they were written by the same individual. In fact, not only were they written the same way – they were both handwritten in pencil – but the same type of paper was used. And that letter was signed "Son of Sam."'

Even more helpful, just supposing that one day Operation Omega closed in on a particular suspect, was the fingerprint evidence. Borelli's letter may have had prints from a variety of careless cops, and Breslin's from a swathe of unsuspecting journalists, but on both there were 21 actual matches – presumably, therefore, those of the author.

Still, no closer to a solution, or an arrest. And the people of New York were jumping to their own apprehensive conclusions. This killer seemed to specialize in young women of a particular appearance: so, as Harvey Schlossberg remembers, 'Everybody was kind of amazed that the victims looked so much like each other, and therefore the solution would be bleach your hair, cut your hair, wear different colours, confuse the killer by making yourself less of a victim' – good news for New York's hairdressers, but not necessarily an insurance policy against Son of Sam.

Indeed, while the publication of the Breslin letter increased general panic – it did, after all, say things like, 'Hello from the cracks in the sidewalks of NYC and from the ants that dwell in these cracks and feed in the dried blood of the dead', and 'Hello from the gutters of NYC, which is filled with dog manure, vomit, stale wine, urine and blood' – the psychologists felt the general hysteria would actually increase the risk. As Schlossberg points out, 'The killer's letters were to aggravate the police and flaunt his achievement in their face – this taunting increases his excitement.'

There was more to the Breslin letter. *News Day*, under instruction from the police, withheld some parts; although, it must be said, neither they nor the police knew quite what to make of them at that stage. They published lines like, 'You must not forget Donna Lauria', which certainly suggested this was from the real killer, but they censored out a very curious passage which only hindsight would be able to explain.

'Here are some names to help you along. Forward them to the Inspector for use by the National Crime Information Center. They have everything on computer, everything. They just might turn up, from some other crimes. Maybe they could make associations. Duke of Death. Wicked King Wicker. The 22 Disciples of Hell. And lastly, John Wheaties, rapist and suffocator of young girls. P.S. drive on, think positive, get off your butts, knock on coffins, etc.'

Nobody ever said that psychopaths should make sense.

In a city where the Mayor is running scared he won't be reelected (and, as a matter of fact, he wasn't), the press and TV are harassing every cop in sight, the women are changing their hairstyles out of panic and the young men can't persuade any girl to drive down lover's lane, the police have to be seen to be doing something. So suddenly, detectives' duties assumed a new dimension. Former NYPD detective Eddie Zigo recollects the time: 'You could drive through any place which was usually a lovers' lane, and it was empty. If you saw a car in there, you could rest assured there was a police officer and a policewoman in that car. We had stake-outs all over the city, and the hysteria was just great – you couldn't imagine.'

In fact, the decoy system had begun with a team of male volunteers sharing their cars with fashion dummies which Borelli had borrowed from contacts in the garment district, but that had proved neither effective bait nor much fun for those assigned.

Borelli wasn't the only one prepared to turn to just about anyone who might conceivably be able to help. The media had been similarly broad-minded in their desperation to flesh out the story, and one psychologist had gone on television to voice his conviction that the killer must be impotent. As Borelli recalls, 'Right after that we got maybe two hundred phone calls from women giving up their impotent boyfriends – we were being inundated with calls, so we had to devise some system. I said that when information came in, the detectives were to take all that information down as they received it and their superior officer, whoever was working, would read it and assign it to one of three boxes – IMMEDIATE, INTER-MEDIATE and FORGET ABOUT IT! And some of the things we put in the last box we never really did anything with.'

That must have worried the methodical Borelli, because one of his very first acts when he ultimately heard that an arrest was imminent was to have that last box searched, just in case the suspect's name had been there all along. To his relief, it wasn't.

That moment was still some way off, however, and Son of Sam, still at large, was ready to strike again. In the early hours of 26 June 1977, Judy Placido and Sal Lupo left a disco in Queens called The Elephas and went to their car. Judy recalls very well what happened next. 'All of a sudden, I heard echoing in the car. There wasn't any pain; just ringing in my ears. I looked at Sal, and his eyes were open wide, just like his mouth. There were no screams. I don't know why I didn't scream. I couldn't understand what this pounding noise was.'

Sal seems to have thought that someone had thrown stones at the car, and got out to run to the disco for help. Judy then saw herself in the mirror – and was horrified to see she was covered in blood. In fact, she'd been lucky – three bullets had hit her, but she had avoided serious injury, while Sal had only been hit once, in the forearm. But while both survived, and could give subjective accounts of what they remembered and imagined, neither could add much of real help to the investigation.

Son of Sam's letter to columnist Jimmy Breslin had only mentioned one victim – Donna Lauria, whom he'd murdered on 29 July 1976. And indeed, in that same letter, the presumed killer had asked: 'Tell me, Jim, what will you have for 29 July?' Although the police were prepared to countenance the notion that he might choose to mark the anniversary by another killing, the media went much further, and effectively paralysed the city with virtual predictions that 29 July 1977 wouldn't be a sensible night to go looking for a secluded parking place.

There are, of course, alternatives and, as was to be cynically observed much later, the only people who might have had regrets when Son of Sam was caught were the motel-owners of the outlying boroughs.

Nevertheless, there were unmarked police cars parked as decoys in as many places as could be managed on the night of 29 July. Nothing happened. But then, Son of Sam – who, as Schlossberg had said, certainly did not want to be caught – presumably read the papers too, and could have guessed that there would be extra vigilance on that date.

He waited, instead, until the small hours of 31 July. Stacy Moskowitz and Bobby Violante had ended their evening date parked near Gravesend Bay in Brooklyn. As Bobby subsequently testified: 'All of a sudden I heard like a humming sound. First I thought I heard glass break. Then I didn't hear Stacy any more. I didn't feel anything, but I saw her fall away from me. I don't know who got shot first: her or me.'

In fact, he had been shot twice, and was to lose his left eye and much of the vision in his right. Stacy had only been shot once, but nothing the surgeons could do was able to save her life.

Now, as Eddy Zigo explains, 'When we have a homicide, standard procedure is to canvass all the people around to see who saw what, who didn't see anything. So in our canvass the next day after Stacy Moskowitz was shot, we were canvassing all these buildings which were right adjacent to the park where the shooting happened and we had many doors just slammed in our faces. The area we were working in is a hub of organized crime people who live there. Most of the major crime families live in that area. So, any time there's a homicide, they figure it's organized crime-connected. I don't like to use the word 'Mafia', but that's what they say: it's Mafia-connected.'

'This went on for two days, and I thought, "It's ridiculous – somebody's got to talk to us", so I just took it upon myself. I went down to a local club they're known to frequent, and I went to see one of the guys who was a head and said, "Look, I have a problem", and told him what it was. I said, "Look, this has nothing to do with your people; as you know, this is a Son of Sam thing. Now it could be your sister, your brother, anybody the next time: all I want is that these people talk to me. They won't talk to me because they're afraid of saying anything to the police." So he said, "All right. Go back to your office; the phones will ring." And sure enough, we went back to our office, and the phones started to ring.'

So the killings had spread from the Bronx, through Queens and now to Brooklyn. In fact, the nearest hospital to Gravesend Bay is the Coney Island Hospital, from where Stacy was sent to the specialist head injury unit at King's

County Hospital, although to no avail. Among the more panicky members of the public, and the Fourth Estate, it began to be feared that it was only a matter of time before Son of Sam moved on to Manhattan and Staten Island. But in fact, everyone, including the Task Force, would have been better advised to switch their attention in quite the opposite direction – up to Yonkers, northwards up the Hudson.

Sam Carr a retired local government official, lived there with his family and their Labrador dog, Harvey. In April 1977, he received two anonymous letters complaining about Harvey's barking. In the second, the writer protested: 'I have asked you kindly to stop that dog from howling all day long, yet he continues to do so. I pleaded with you. I told you how this is destroying my family. We have no peace – no rest. Now I know what kind of person you are and what kind of family you are. You are cruel and inconsiderate. You have no love for any other human beings. You're selfish, Mr Carr. My life is destroyed now. I have nothing to lose any more. I can see that there shall be no peace in my life, or my families life, until I end yours.'

Understandably, the Carrs called the local police, but they couldn't – didn't – offer much save sympathy. Then, at the end of the month, the Carrs heard a gunshot in their yard. Sam Carr rushed out to find his dog bleeding from a wound, and in time to catch a glimpse of a man wearing jeans and a yellow shirt making his escape.

Fortunately, the vet was able to save Harvey, and after this incident the local police took more of an interest. In fact, they took the two letters off for examination – but since Captain Borelli's own anonymous letter was being kept secret on a need-to-know basis even within Operation Omega, there was no reason for a Yonkers officer to imagine that threatening letters from anonymous psychos were possibly of any wider interest.

Some six weeks later, and again well upstate of the city in New Rochelle, Jack Cassara was puzzled to get a get-well card in the mail. It purported to come from someone called Carr in Yonkers, and contained a photograph of an Alsatian dog. The message was quite bizarre: 'Dear Jack, I'm sorry to hear about that fall you took from the roof of your house. Just want to say "I'm sorry" but I'm sure it won't be long until you feel much better, healthy, well and strong. Please be careful next time. Since you're going to be confined for a long time, let us know if Nann needs anything. Sincerely, Sam and Francis.'

Bizarre – because Cassara had not fallen off his roof, and had never heard of Sam and Francis Carr. Puzzled, he rang them – and when they immediately said that they too had received worrying anonymous letters, it was agreed that Jack and Nann Cassara would drive over to Yonkers that very evening. The Carrs not only told the story of Harvey's shooting, but cast light on the photograph: apparently another dog, this time an Alsatian, had also been shot, on nearby Wicker Street.

Sam Carr's daughter, Wheat, worked as a dispatcher for the Yonkers police, and she promptly passed on this fresh information to her colleagues who had investigated the earlier complaint. Similarly, the Cassaras filed a report with their local New Rochelle police, while their teenage son Stephen added a thought of his own – recalling a short-stay tenant who had taken a room in their house the previous year, and had been unreasonably bothered by their dog. That, too, was given to both police forces; so in Yonkers and New Rochelle, at least, it was on record that a man called David Berkowitz might be implicated in sending threatening letters, and in shooting dogs.

None of this might reasonably have been expected to ring an alarm bell labelled 'Son of Sam.' Every police force in the world has files on nuisance neighbours, very few of whom ever turn out to be serial killers. However, the Yonkers force did open a file on Berkowitz, and log the licence-plate number of his Ford Galaxy car, plus the fact that his licence had just been suspended.

Ignorant of all this, the NYPD was still following every hunch on offer. Quite reasonably, Borelli conjectured that since every killing had taken place near a main arterial road or highway, it was worth checking through summonses. 'We figured, you know, he jumps in his car,' says Joe Borelli, 'he's speeding away, may be he's got a summons for reckless driving or speeding. And then we started checking the bridges, cutting off traffic at the bridges and all. So when Stacy Moskowitz got killed, they closed down the bridges: they had cops on the bridges. We found out later that Berkowitz sat in the park reading the newspaper, and he was heading back upstate to Yonkers and was on the Triborough

Bridge and they were stopping cars, and then it got to be like nine or ten o'clock in the morning and they called it off. They missed him by about three or four cars.'

Summonses were a good idea – but not for speeding, jumping red lights or reckless driving. Several days after the Moskowitz/Violante shooting, a Brooklyn resident called Cecile Davis finally plucked up her courage to go to the police and tell them she thought she might have seen the killer when walking her dog late at night. She had spotted a man lurking behind a tree in the park, who'd then seemed to follow her: frightened, and subsequently claiming that she thought she'd seen a gun in his hand, she'd hurried home and, just as she was removing her dog Snowball's collar, had heard 'something that sounded like firecrackers – kind of loud, but far off.'

She didn't learn what had happened a block away from her door until the following morning, and then, 'I realized I must have seen the killer. I panicked, and I couldn't say anything. I would never forget his face. It was frightening.' Yet even when she overcame her fear and approached the police, they were sceptical. Her description of the killer's clothing didn't match that of another witness who'd been parked near Bobby Violante's car, and she then insisted that despite the very late hour, she had seen police officers issuing parking tickets on her street. Yet the investigating officers had already thought of that possibility, and been told that no such tickets were issued in that area that night.

Pressed, Mrs Davis actually described the two patrolmen

she claimed to have seen. Fortunately, her information was classified under IMMEDIATE rather than FORGET ABOUT IT, and her description of the ticket-issuing cops was checked with the local precinct. Yes, there had indeed been two officers on that shift who had, it now emerged, written a ticket for double-parking. In fact, it had already been paid.

A rapid trawl through the files turned up just one such ticket, issued to the owner of a Ford Galaxy, whose address was up in Yonkers – a David Berkowitz. One of the investigating officers made a preliminary call to the Yonkers police, almost as a professional courtesy, to say they'd be coming up into their patch to interview a potential witness (which is all that could be inferred at that time), a Mr Berkowitz. And as Joe Borelli remembers, they suddenly got lucky. The call was taken by Wheat Carr, and the moment she heard the name, says Joe, 'She got all excited – "Oh, he's a psycho!" And she's whetting the appetite of the detectives, right?'

Suddenly, things started falling into place. The Yonkers police were able to make sense of quite a lot of the puzzle. For example, in Breslin's letter, 'Wicked King Wicker' plainly came from the Yonkers street-name, and 'John Wheaties' connected to Wheat Carr. More urgently, Yonkers revealed they were currently investigating a suspected arson at the apartment block where Berkowitz lived. A neighbour of his, Craig Glassman, a part-time sheriff's deputy, had smelled smoke at his door and, when he opened it, discovered a smouldering fire into which a number of .22 bullets had been put. What's more, Glassman had shown the police letters he had received from Berkowitz, which they noticed strongly resembled the letters the Carrs had received.

In one of those letters, the author actually wrote: 'True, I am the killer, but Craig, the killings are at your command.' The Yonkers police had actually relayed that information to the Task Force as soon as they got it – but it had mysteriously been treated as INTERMEDIATE, just as had a personal visit from Sam Carr to the Omega office a couple of days earlier.

Now, however, everybody involved had promoted the weird Mr Berkowitz to IMMEDIATE.

Detectives John Falotico and Eddy Zigo drove up to Yonkers on 10 August 1977. As Zigo got closer to the address on the parking ticket, he recalls: 'I'm starting to get that feeling, so I said to John, "Let's look for the car", and sure enough we spot the car. We look at it – empty, clean, locked – and in the back seat there was a dufflebag, an Army dufflebag, so I said to my partner to go back to our car; I wanted to check it out. And I managed to get into the car – he must have left the window a little ajar – and I was able to get into it.' (Whether the window had been ajar or not, it can be assumed that an experienced cop, with or without a search warrant, would have had little difficulty in finding his way into a very common, and relatively cheap, model of car.)

'Well', says Eddy, 'I looked in that dufflebag, and the first thing I saw was the butt of an automatic weapon, and I pulled it out, and he had the Army clips, military-style, taped together, and they were fully loaded. There were 35 rounds in each clip and he had seven of them. So I put that back: that's not what I wanted, but it's there. So now I go into the dash compartment and there were pictures, the sort you take in those booths, so now I know what David Berkowitz looks like, but still nothing. Now I go under the front seat and I find this letter and I pulled it out very gingerly and I looked at it and it's addressed to the New York press and to the Police Department, so I took it out and read it, and now my partner comes back, and I'm reading it, and before you know it my whole body was shaking... and John asked me what was wrong, and I said: "John, we got him – this is him. This is the letter he's going to drop at the next scene – he's just stated it all." So I put it all back in, locked the car up, and went back to our car, and we sat there.'

Zigo radioed back to base with his information and to ask for extra back-up, plus search warrants. As they waited, a man came out of the apartment block, Number 35 Pine Street, and appeared to head towards the Galaxy. The cops closed in on him with guns drawn – only to discover that it was Deputy Sheriff Craig Glassman, who quickly spotted that these were not Yonkers cops at all, but from New York. And he equally quickly worked out what and whom they were after.

Nevertheless, it was an hour or two more before the second, heavy-set, dark-haired white male left the building. This time, the growing number of police watchers waited until he'd actually got into the car before surrounding it, and while John Falotico held a gun to his head, Eddy Zigo asked: 'Are you Mr Berkowitz?'

'And that's when he turned round', says Zigo, 'looked at me, smiled, and said: "No. I'm the Son of Sam."'

Backed this time with his legitimate search warrant, Zigo went through the car again – 'and that's when I came up with the .44 calibre gun' he remembers. 'And the Inspector says. "Did you get the gun?" Because without the gun we had nobody – he could have been a crank – and I says I got the gun and he says, "What does it say – what does it say?" and I said, "Well, it says .44 – Charter Arms .44 calibre."'

By now everybody from Yonkers right downtown to City Hall and Police HQ had heard the news, and the excitement was mounting. Inevitably, everybody wanted to get in on the act of producing the prime suspect before the reporters and the cameras, from Mayor Beame to the Police Commissioner to Dowd and all his colleagues. In fact, Joe Borelli remembers saying to the Mayor, '"You know there's a ban? We can't drink alcohol beverages in police facilities", and he said. "Really? I just did away with that ban", and he reached into his pocket and took out two $100 bills and said. "Go and get some refreshments."'

The arresting officers, and rather a lot of others, effectively formed a motorcade to bring Son of Sam down from Yonkers to Police Plaza. Zigo was still in a state of some shock, for when he'd gone to search Berkowitz's apartment he'd found a loaded pump-action shotgun just inside the door. When he returned, he mentioned it to Berkowitz, and asked him, 'What if I'd come knocking at that door – would you have done me?' All he did was smile – and I said, 'You would have.'

The sense of relief was enormous. Dating all across the city reverted to being a favourite pastime, rather than a high-risk activity, and the police, with the gun, the letters, the prints, knew that even if their witnesses were shaky, the forensic science looked good. But Berkowitz – by no means unexpectedly, in the circumstances – was quite aware that his best hope probably lay in an insanity defence. He was referred to Danny Schwarz, then director of the Forensic Psychiatry Service at King's County Hospital. His job, he explains, was 'primarily to examine criminal defendants as to their fitness to proceed: that is, whether they had any degree of mental illness, and if so, whether this impaired their abilities to understand the charges against them and assist in their defence; second, to advise the courts as to what might be the best sentence; and thirdly, we had a treatment service for those still being held in jail.'

As it happened, Schwarz and his colleagues did report their view that Berkowitz's 'beliefs, delusions, prevented him from entering a rational defence, because he was so psychotic he believed in his delusions, and he would therefore not take up the defence of insanity because, to him, this was not insanity but reality.' It was a subtle professional point, but neither the District Attorney nor the judge for the preliminary hearing, actually held in the hospital, bought it.

At this point Berkowitz, who had already confessed in some detail, really had no further choice but to plead guilty. He was arraigned on 23 August 1977, and sentenced to 365 years in prison.

Having been terrorized for a year, some New Yorkers promptly demonstrated why some people find the city perplexing. They flocked up to Yonkers in search of souvenirs from Son of Sam's run-down and squalid apartment. A quarter of the other tenants in the building moved out in despair – and the landlord got permission to change the street number to confuse the ghouls.

ANGELO BUONO AND KENNETH BIANCHI –
THE HILLSIDE STRANGLERS

Yolanda Washington was nobody. A street whore in Los Angeles, of Afro-American descent, found naked, raped and strangled on a hillside near Forest Lawn cemetery doesn't excite the police, and doesn't even make the papers. Girls like her turned up dead, by murder or by overdose, every week. As Frank Salerno of the Sheriff's Department said, 'It's not that unusual an occurrence here, unfortunately, to discover a murdered female that's been dumped somewhere in the city or the county.'

So 17 October 1977 was just another day in everyone's diary but Yolanda's: no panic, no fuss, no coverage and no great interest.

Come to that, there was really no great excitement when the world-weary Frank Salerno was called out on 30 October to La Crescenta, north of Glendale, where another naked female body, this time white, had been found. She, too, had been strangled: she, too, had been raped, sodomized and murdered elsewhere, and then deliberately dumped on a middle-class hillside site.

Nevertheless, Salerno did a professional job. He noted not just that she was small and thin, apparently around 16 years old, but that there were marks of ligatures on both ankles and wrists, as well as her throat. Furthermore, on her eyelid was a small piece of light fluff. It might be a clue, but not one that would lead to a suspect: just one which might help if there was ever a suspect in mind.

But what really struck the detective was that, however light the body may have been, the complete absence of drag-marks on the soil or the victim strongly suggested that she had been carried off the road – and very possibly by two men, not one.

Despite her youth, nobody seemed to have filed a Missing Persons report on her, so Salerno started working the streets around Hollywood Boulevard, then widely recognized as the natural haven for dropouts, runaways, addicts and whores. One name cropped up repeatedly as he showed his grim portrait around – Judy Miller. And, yes, she too had been a street prostitute: so, yet again, no great publicity, no widespread interest and, frankly, no particular pressure on the police. As a colleague remarked, 'Frank was chasing – this is just another street hooker with no hope in sight.'

Still, the press had actually noticed this time – 'Two Glendale Slayings May Be Linked' said the tiny story on page 27 of the *Los Angeles Times* of 10 November.

ANGELO BUONO AND KENNETH BIANCHI

In fact, it took a third murder for even Frank Salerno to start seriously worrying that a serial killer, or killers, might be at work. Lissa Kastin, a 21-year-old waitress at the Healthfaire Restaurant near Hollywood and Vine, turned out to have mentioned to her mother that she was considering prostitution to earn some extra money, but she wasn't actually turning tricks: she was white, was quickly identified – and the Glendale police who found her near a country club on Sunday, 6 November 1977, spotted and reported the same five-point ligature marks which showed on Yolanda Washington and Judy Miller. What's more, when Salerno visited the site after talking to the Glendale force, he noted that a substantial guardrail between the road and the hillside strongly supported his surmise that two men, not one, must have been involved.

What began at Hallowe'en as just another killing of a prostitute finally became front-page news in Thanksgiving week. Three curiously similar murders in a month or so is, sadly, nothing special in Los Angeles, of which Sergeant Bob Grogan of the Los Angeles Police Department has since remarked: 'It was full of crazy sons of bitches in the '70s – it seems that every wacko, every disenfranchised idiot in the country came to LA. We were the melting pot of the world for wackos.'

But when five new victims – one 12, one 14 and all of them 'nice girls' – turn up on neighbouring hillsides in the week of America's classic celebration of national and family pride, even Los Angeles begins to panic.

The first call came to Bob Grogan of the LAPD on Sunday,

20 November. He'd been hoping to enjoy his day off with his family, not least because his relationship with his wife was beginning to come under strain – and he was drinking most of a bottle of Scotch a day. Still, he had no choice but to drive out to a remote hillside location near Eagle Rock, where he saw the body of Kristina Weckler, naked, obviously raped and sodomized and, as Grogan spotted automatically, bearing the signs of the five-point ligature. Still ignorant of what Frank Salerno had already seen and surmised, Grogan also formed the immediate theory that the murder had taken place some-where else, and that it had very possibly taken two men who knew the area well to carry the body off the road.

And curiously, although Kristina showed none of the track-marks of the habitual heroin addict, the autopsy noted just two puncture marks on her arm.

But what really set alarm bells ringing city-wide, across all the different city and county investigating forces, was the call to Grogan's partner, Detective Dudley Varney, later that same day. On the other side of that same hill, Varney discov-ered two bodies, dumped on a local trash heap. They were Dolores Cepeda, 12, and Sonja Johnson, 14, both of whom had been reported missing for a week from St Ignatius School and had last been seen getting off a bus and talking to two men in a large two-tone saloon car.

Kristina Weckler, 20, was an honours student at the Pasadena Art Centre of Design. Dolores Cepeda and Sonja Johnson were well-brought up schoolgirls of Mexican origin. The police, the press and the public could no longer ignore these murders as something that didn't affect decent families.

On the other hand, all the similarities which linked these six murders were negative from the police viewpoint. No clothing or jewellery in the vicinity. Common marks of ligatures – but no ropes or tape still present. No fingerprints, no tyre-marks, no drag marks or footprints. No witnesses. And as Bob Grogan explained, 'If you don't have a murder scene, that's one of the biggest problems – you're really in trouble because your forensics and your evidence that will point you towards the murder and how the murder was committed are non-existent. We didn't have a murder scene: all we had was locations where people were found. So instead of starting at A, you're kind of starting at D, and working backwards instead of going forward with your investigation.'

What's more, it's easy nowadays to forget how very recently the business of detection has benefited from new technologies. Grogan, Salerno and their colleagues couldn't look to DNA to make their case against any eventual suspect, nor even expect computers to take most of the humdrum burden of processing evidence.

As Grogan said: 'God, I wish we had DNA and computers then. We would probably have saved three women's lives.' Because when a fourth body was discovered in that same week, – that of Jane King, who had been lying near the Los Feliz off-ramp of the Golden State Freeway for around two weeks – the investigators had four bodies inside a few days, but three different sites covered by three different detectives.

ANGELO BUONO AND KENNETH BIANCHI

Grogan again: 'So the information doesn't start flowing back and forth – like, this is the pre-computer age, where everything and anything was documented and hand-written. I mean, we got writer's cramp writing some of this stuff down. Well, you send that teletype out – "Does anybody have any murder similar to this?" Well, every woman who's ever been strangled we got a response to, and that overwhelms you – you can't deal with that shit.'

Still, experienced detectives could still make certain assumptions on the evidence of their eyes. In Grogan's words, 'This has gotta be a son of a bitch. This is not gonna be the guy next door, this is not gonna be the jealous boyfriend or the husband or the girlfriend, this is not gonna be over dope or money: this is gonna be a son of a bitch.'

But experienced detectives could also come up with an even more distressing theory. Among all those things which linked the murders by their absence was this: none of the bodies bore the usual marks of resistance – no black eyes, no bruises, scratches, skin under fingernails, defence wounds on hands or forearms. In other words, all these young women had submitted to being restrained, bound, stripped, without putting up a fight.

'What does that tell you ?' asked Bob Grogan. 'A figure of authority. We got a couple of cops doing this shit. Isn't that wonderful? I mean, we got a shit case to work, with no clues, but now we may be looking at investigating two police officers, so that really adds to your pressure.'

And the pressure was rapidly going off the scale. After the

discovery of Jane King's body, the authorities desperately set up a special task force, initially with 30 officers drawn from the LAPD, the Sheriff's Department and the Glendale Police Department. It was soon to grow to around 100 – or, as Grogan said, 'a hundred amateurs. When you go out and ask division Captains to send men down to a task force, they don't send their best guys down. You know, everybody knows that: you don't have to be a genius to figure it out. So what do you get? You get guys that they don't want working. I mean, I'm not going to bad-mouth anybody I work with, but we had some shit-heads – we had some people who were totally incompetent investigating clues.'

Frank Salerno took a similar view, but with greater restraint. 'Investigation by committee doesn't work – Captains and Commanders of stations were told to send six or eight or whatever number of investigators to the task force, no questions asked: that's what you're ordered to do. Well, naturally they didn't always send their best people down, because they had their own problems to handle.' But as Frank also remarked, 'Bob Grogan is an individual that likes to fly by the seat of his pants, while I'd describe myself as being a little more methodical, a little more laid-back in my approach.'

What both nevertheless recall is that the moment their anxious bosses set up the Task Force, and let the media know not just about the links between the murders but that it was possible the perpetrator might be a rogue policeman, the clues came flooding in. Grogan's estimate is that something like

11,500 separate pieces of information came in in three months, all of which had to be checked out – if only to eliminate them.

And to be fair, the swelling pack of detectives were now given a large, and fairly primitive, computer to process their burgeoning heap of data: PATRIC, or Pattern Recognition and Information Correlation, met with Grogan's customary cynicism. 'That's all we need. It's nothing but a fifty-thousand-dollar filing cabinet.'

And there was now panic in the streets. Barely had the people of greater Los Angeles been told there was a task force investigating what seemed to be a series of murders than yet another one was discovered. Immediately after the Thanksgiving weekend, Grogan was called to the hills around Mount Washington. The naked body of Lauren Wagner, an 18-year-old student who lived with her parents in the San Fernando Valley, was found partially in the street, the five-point ligature, absence of clothes and drag-marks conforming to the established pattern. According to the media, who were not being told of the strong presumption that there were two killers, the Hillside Strangler had struck again.

Sales of guns, large dogs, security locks and courses in self-defense took off. Parents, including Grogan, lectured their daughters on the folly of doing almost anything which daughters might want to do. None of them, cops included, had any real idea what or who might specifically offer the greatest threat. But in this case there were three extra clues for the detectives to explore.

First, Lauren's hands bore what seemed to be burn marks.

Second, although the killers had removed the adhesive tape which had bound her wrists, a fair amount of the gum itself had adhered to Lauren's skin – and adhering to that, in turn, there was a tuft of fibres. As Katherine Vukovich of the Sheriff's crime lab explained: 'Usually when you go out to crime scenes you find maybe two to five fibres, and they're usually of the same type, usually cotton or polyester or whatever. On Lauren's right wrist, the tuft contained 403 fibres, the majority of them acrylic, and there were about 12 different types. There were also 29 nylon fibres, five of them from a Monsanto plant that was no longer in production.' Tremendous – but only if you knew, or suspected, where Lauren had been when her wrists were bound.

Third, there was a witness to her abduction – which took place immediately outside her parents' home as she parked her Mustang car on the street. Neighbour Beulah Stofer's Doberman dog had barked at about nine o'clock in the evening of 28 November, and Beulah had looked for the cause. What she told Grogan she had seen was a large dark car with a white top pull up behind Lauren's and two men dragging the girl into it, as she screamed, 'You won't get away with this!'

Beulah Stofer was in her late 50s, an asthmatic, and claimed she had seen all this – she described two men, one tall and young with acne scars, the other older, shorter and Latin-looking – from inside her house. What's more, she had thought it was just a quarrel. It was to turn out that she had not only been traumatized by the event, having been raped as a young woman herself, but had been telephoned the following day by a man with a New York accent who, having established that she was 'the woman with a dog', told her to keep her mouth shut or he would kill her.

Still, that car, with its two-tone paint job resembling a police patrol vehicle, and the brazen way the abductors had stopped and 'arrested' Lauren, reinforced the theory that the perpetrators might be masquerading as policemen. All California cops were well aware that their state had been home to Caryl Chessman, the 'red-light bandit', who had been convicted in 1948 after using a red light on his car to persuade couples parked in secluded spots to open their car doors, at which point he showed them a pistol and forced the female into his own car, where he sexually assaulted her. Subsequently, of course, he went on to become one of America's best-known inhabitants of Death Row, fighting a protracted battle from his cell to avoid the then-penalty for his crimes.

The cops were not alone. Someone else in Los Angeles had taken careful note of Chessman's scam.

Angelo Buono was born in Rochester, New York, on 5 October 1934, but moved to Glendale, California, with his divorced mother in 1939. The family was of Sicilian descent, but Angelo signally failed to show his mother the devoted respect which that background might suggest. On the other hand, he certainly conformed to another stereotype, earning his first conviction for stealing a car as he entered his teens, and boasting to his schoolmates about raping and sodomizing girls: his attitude to women was to remain uniformly brutal and exploitative, as one might imagine from his chilling habit of calling even his mother a 'c**t'.

By 1977 Buono had run through several marriages, and fathered at least eight children. All of his wives and children were abused, at least physically, and in several cases sexually. Yet Buono was kind to animals – he had a tank of angel-fish, a hutch of rabbits and a devoted yard-dog – and obsessively tidy about the house. His collections – of men's magazines, Zippo lighters, antique model cars and guns (five rifles, two .45 pistols and a Tommy gun, which reminds us that a string of criminal convictions and civil contempts is no bar to owning deadly weapons in some places) – were all immaculately kept and displayed.

Now living on his own next to his automobile upholstery shop, Buono was a classic loner, except that in late 1975 the adopted son of some cousins back in Rochester arrived in California and turned to Angelo at first for lodging, and then for leadership. Kenny Bianchi was 17 years younger than Buono, but had already left a failed marriage behind and lost a series of jobs as a security guard when employers noted that their stock losses seemed higher when Kenny was on guard than when he was not.

While both shared a wholly exploitative contempt for women, Kenny added something extra to the mix. Angelo seems to have had a powerful sexual magnetism, but was both ugly and unpolished. Kenny, on the other hand, was not only better-looking, but had a glib charm which he could apparently turn on at will. All too many of the women he had

ANGELO BUONO AND KENNETH BIANCHI

known used the same expression about Kenny: 'He was like a used car salesman.'

Which gave Angelo a great idea. They would set up in the pimping business. Kenny could find the girls and he, Angelo, would find the customers. Meantime both, of course, would enjoy endless free sex from their string.

Kenny's first recruit was a 16-year old girl from Phoenix, Arizona, who had come to Los Angeles, she told him at a party, to look for modelling work. Naturally, he told her how lucky she was – he had amazing contacts in that very business, and could virtually guarantee her an easy $500 a week. Sabra Hannan told him she was off to visit friends in Lubbock, Texas, then on briefly back to Phoenix, but would think it over.

When Sabra rang Bianchi from Phoenix, having thought it over, she fell right into the trap. She didn't, she said, have the air fare to come back to LA, but if Kenny could advance the money, she could pay him back out of her first $500. Oh, and if he could find her somewhere to stay for the first few days...

It didn't take the cousins very long to convince poor Sabra that if she didn't provide them, and anyone else they suggested, with sexual services, she would bitterly regret it. Angelo's long experience as a wife- and child-beater had taught him that a bath-towel soaked in water could not only inflict pain, but left no bruises.

There was no shortage of business. Indeed, Angelo noticed that his core business – the automobile upholstery shop – started picking up extra custom when word got around that instead of drinking stale coffee and leafing through old magazines while waiting for your car to be fixed, you could enjoy a modelling session with Sabra.

And when Angelo was asked if he could supply girls for an afternoon orgy at a cardboard factory in Cudahy, in the south-east of Los Angeles County, he bullied one of his own lovers, Antoinette Lombardo, a high-school senior who had already undergone an abortion to prove her devotion to him, into joining the team. As the customers included both a local councillor and the police chief of a small nearby town, it was essential to give good service.

But Antoinette couldn't be counted on at all times – she did, after all, have to go to school. So the cousins graciously allowed Sabra to make a quick trip back home to Phoenix – provided she returned with a new recruit. Since Angelo had managed to convince her that he was a Mafiosi, and that the local Mob would be keeping a watchful eye on her in Arizona, she needn't think of doing anything but returning.

Astonishingly, she did, and with a 15-year-old friend in tow. Rebekah Gay Spears was scarcely an innocent; since Sabra didn't have their air fare, both girls turned tricks at the Phoenix Airport to raise the money. Neverthless, sexual enslavement to Angelo and Kenny can scarcely have been what she had in mind when she told Sabra that she was looking forward to a new life in California.

But that is exactly what she got. Becky was installed in Angelo's spare room, Sabra in a nearby apartment, and both were added to the roster of the Foxy Ladies call-girl service, so that having obliged Angelo, Kenny and Angelo's customers during the day, they could be profitably despatched around the city in the evenings. And one night in August 1977 a lawyer in affluent Bel-Air named David Wood called Foxy Ladies to ask for a house-call.

When Becky Spears arrived, she seemed so pathetic and wretched that Wood asked her the question most whores take in their stride: 'How did you get into this?' And Becky told him the grisly truth, with vivid details about Angelo, Kenny, their lies and threats. The lawyer was horrified, and instead of waiting for the Foxy Ladies driver to arrive and take Becky back to slavery, he arranged for her to catch the first plane back to Phoenix in the morning.

When Becky failed to return, Angelo tracked her last call and very foolishly began to threaten Wood. Successful lawyers can, however, call in favours from grateful clients, and the consequence of Buono's threats was a surprise visit to his upholstery shop by a 300-pound bouncer called Tiny, accompanied by four equally intimidating colleagues. A brief and pointed exchange ensured that whatever else he did, Angelo wasn't going to utter any more threats against David Wood.

As if that wasn't bad enough for the cousins' amour-propre, the next month Sabra managed to escape, and skipped the state. Not only no more sex on tap, but a sharp drop in income: and their rage at Becky and Sabra's desertion began to foment a more general rage against not just whores, but women in general.

Now at this stage, of course, the task force had no real lead at all: just things which would possibly fall into place when they had a suspect or suspects. Naturally, with all the publicity, others were eager to offer the police the benefit of their talents. Psychiatrists told them that such killers customarily hated their mothers, leading Grogan to observe, 'Gee – all we gotta do now is find a male who hates his mother. Can't be many of those around!' And a private detective from Berlin flew in from Germany, at his own expense, to tell the investigators they should be looking for two Italians – brothers – aged about 35.

Naturally, the cops didn't place any reliance on that – how could a man who didn't even speak English, and knew nothing of the case more than the fragments of news which had percolated as far as the German press, be expected to solve a mystery which had so far defeated a hundred California detectives? Sadly, nobody seems to have gone back to the psychic Berliner later to ask him how and why he had got so close to a profile of cousins Buono and Bianchi.

He certainly didn't know, any more than Grogan and Salerno, that Kenny drove a big Cadillac with a blue body and white top, that Angelo Buono much admired Caryl Chessman and owned both a police badge and a pair of hand-cuffs, and that Kenny entertained lasting fantasies about joining the police.

So, while the task force laboriously ploughed on through the thousands of 'clues', Buono and Bianchi were free to continue their murderous career. After eight victims in two months they seemed to take a rest, something which arouses very mixed emotions in policemen in pursuit of serial killers: nobody, obviously, wants there to be another victim, but if the inquiry isn't apparently getting anywhere, cops know that if there is a next one, this could be the time the killer makes a mistake, and gives them the lead they lack. As Grogan admits, 'When he stops killing, you're in trouble – when the murders stop, the information stops flowing.'

And in mid-December, there was the next one. Laid out on a steep hillside on Alvarado Street was the body of Kimberly Diane Martin, a tall, blonde call-girl, whose last client had summoned her to Apartment 114 at 1950 Tamarind, which turned out to be vacant. Now 'escort services' routinely check on the number from which a client calls, for very sensible reasons, and never send one of their girls out if the phone used is a public one: yet in this case, although the call had been made from a pay-phone in the lobby of the Hollywood Public Library and there was no phone listed for the address on Tamarind, they had – which strongly suggested that the client, and thus very probably the murderer, had a very persuasive manner indeed. Or, as Grogan was to put it later, 'Bianchi's got a line of bullshit 83 miles long. That's how smart this ass is.'

Now, finger-printing a public callbox is plainly a very long shot, but the investigation had no real option but to clutch at any straw on offer. So the technicians lifted every print they could get from the pay-phone,and added them to the files. Yet another possible clue, if and when there was a suspect to match them to – and when, eventually, they had one, it was to turn out that among those prints were those of Kenny Bianchi.

For the rest of December, all through January and for the first fortnight of February 1978 there were no more victims. But on 17 February a Datsun car was spotted down the slope of a hillside on Angeles Crest. In the trunk was the strangled and violated body of Cindy Hudspeth, a popular 20-year old clerk who had last been seen the previous afternoon in her apartment building at 800, East Garfield Avenue – which is just across the street from where Kristina Weckler had lived. Another fleeting neighbour later proved to have been Kenny Bianchi.

As soon as the detectives from the Sheriff's department opened the trunk and saw Cindy, they called the task force. The nudity, the five-point ligature, the hillside location – the signs were unmistakable. And from the police viewpoint, after some eight weeks' silence – well, to quote Bob Grogan, 'You almost hate to say it, but it was like, "Goddam: here we go. We're back in the game – we've got a chance."'

But it was Cindy Hudspeth's own car,and nothing in it or about it seemed to offer a lead to anyone else.

And then – silence. As the months of 1978 went by without any further Hillside stranglings, the task force was gradually wound down, leaving only Frank Salerno and Bob Grogan fully committed. As Salerno says, 'The clues were fairly well run out, and our department got back to the regular rotation of handling other murders, and that went on until January of 1979.'

Grogan wasn't that unhappy about the dismantling of the task force. 'We always felt we had to re-do all the investigations that were done by a lot of members of the task force. We felt that there weren't a lot of people with a lot of expertise doing these investigations, and it was our position that we would have to re-do them all anyhow, so that's where we started: we started doing what had already been done.'

He didn't know it at the time, but his jaundiced view of his departing colleagues was more than justified. Kenny Bianchi had been staying for a while with some acquaintances on Corona Street. In February 1978 they kicked him out, having lost patience with his irregular habits, failure to pay rent, borrowing their cars without permission, asking in high school students to smoke dope and showing pornographic movies. Kenny wasn't an ideal tenant. What's more, he seemed to be in possession of a California Highway Patrol badge, which seemed worrying in the light of the media coverage of the Hillside Strangler's supposed impersonation of an officer. So when Kenny had gone, his former flatmates mentioned the badge to a Glendale policeman.

Another Glendale officer went to call on Bianchi at his new apartment, and asked if he had such a badge. Kenny denied it, and the officer took his word. Shortly afterwards, two LAPD officers came to call: a Mrs Wanda Kellison, whose daughter Sheryl had started dating Kenny, didn't like the look of him at all and had rung the task force to say she had this feeling he might be the Strangler. The man with an 83-mile long line of bullshit had no difficulty in disarming them, and they filed a routine report implying that lots of mothers didn't like the men their daughters dated.

Besides, Kenny had told them of his ambition, if not to join the police, then to become a police reserve, and that he'd already put in an application – as, indeed, he had. On that application, there was a full set of his fingerprints, but the investigating officers didn't even know that PATRIC had records of prints from the Tamarind apartment and the Public Library pay-phone. Nor did they know that one of Kenny's previous addresses was on Tamarind, and that he had previously had a routine neighbourhood interview there with task force officers.

And they didn't know – how could they? – that when Kenny was trying to join the Police Reserve, he had gone on two patrol-car rides, and asked the accompanying Sergeant if he could see the Hillside Strangler crime scenes: although the request was refused for security reasons, it hadn't been reported. One can see why Bob Grogan and Frank Salerno took a jaundiced view of investigation by committee.

Grogan's instincts and experience were nagging away at him as the months slipped by with no new murders. 'You start thinking like them (the murderers)' he explains, 'and at this point in time the advantage we had is that we're talking about two guys – definitely, absolutely two guys – and two guys can never keep a secret. One serial murderer's tough to catch: two serial murderers working together shouldn't be that much of a problem because they're gonna get pissed off with each other. Something's gonna happen, the relationship's gonna deteriorate, and we're gonna get the advantage of that.'

He was absolutely right. Kenny not only couldn't resist telling flatmates about his badge, showing an excessive interest in the stranglings to girlfriends, virtually taunting the police on ride-alongs – he also couldn't resist telling Angelo about his cleverness, and his successful handling of investigators.

Angelo was furious. It didn't seem to have occurred to Kenny that three interviews with the cops might suggest they knew rather more than they were letting on, and that giving them both a free set of your fingerprints and expressing special interest in the Hillside stranglings might close the net. Angelo Buono couldn't know that absolutely no connections had been made, and that random interviews with Kenny were lost in the 11,500-clue limbo of PATRIC, even if they had got that far. What he did know was that getting caught because his cousin had far too big a mouth was not any part of his cold-blooded game plan.

Being Angelo, the answer was succinct. He showed Kenny one of his pistols, bawled him out and told him to get lost, or he'd kill him.

Throughout March and April, Angelo ignored Kenny's calls, and, as if drawing a line under their partnership, actually got married again. He certainly seems to have toyed with the notion of killing his former partner but, being careful Angelo, worked out that while nobody had managed to make links between him and the strangled girls, the link between the cousins Bianchi and Buono would very rapidly be picked up. So when Kenny told him that his regular girlfriend, Kelli Boyd, had left him, and taken their young son Ryan up to her parents' home town of Bellingham, Washington, Angelo urged him to go and join her.

Kenny didn't act on the hint for another month, so Angelo made the position very blunt indeed: a new life with Kelli up towards the Canadian border – or a bullet in California.

If you're threatened quite so explicitly by a man who you know, better than anyone else possibly could, regards murder as an evening's relaxation, it concentrates the mind. Kenny went off to Bellingham, where he not only got a job as a security guard but was accepted into the Whatcom County Sheriff's Reserves, and began attending classes in police procedure.

Angelo married Tai Fun Fanny Leung, a 21-year-old Hong Kong citizen who wanted the right of residence in the United States, and whose parents were sending her money to buy a house, which Angelo reckoned he could easily grab.

The task force wound steadily down, as no new clues and no new crimes came in.

And it looked more and more as if the Hillside Strangler(s) had got clean away with it.

Except that Kenny, rather than Angelo, seems to have missed the perverted thrill of rape and murder. There were compensations. His first job in Washington State had allowed him to fill his new home with goods stolen from Fred Meyer's hardware and variety store, and his second, as a roving security man for Whatcom Security Agency Inc., had brought both a company pick-up truck and the opportunity to have business cards printed announcing him to be 'Captain Kenneth Bianchi, Operations Supervisor'; but, fundamentally, Bellingham and Kelli both bored him. Bellingham was a strait-laced, wholesome town of barely 40,000 inhabitants north of Seattle: Kelli was, in his eyes, no longer desirable since she had given birth. On the other hand, Captain Bianchi did have access to a wide range of properties: empty holiday homes whose owners had contracted with Whatcom Security for out-of-season coverage.

When Kelli decided yet again that this relationship was not really made in Heaven and asked Kenny if he would consider moving out after Christmas 1978, Bianchi seems to have tipped, and decided to show Kelli, Bellingham and far-away Angelo Buono that he was someone to be taken seriously.

On Tuesday, 9 January 1979, Kenny telephoned Karen Mandic, a student he had met while working at Fred Meyer's store. His call was answered by her room-mate, Diane Wilder. Bianchi asked her to get Karen to call him. When she did, he offered her a house-sitting job on one of his empty properties which, he said, was having a new burglar-alarm fitted, and would therefore be temporarily vulnerable for the coming Thursday night. The pay would be a hundred dollars and, by the way, why didn't she bring Diane along to keep her company overnight? Oh – and best not to mention this to anyone other than Diane, since his clients mightn't be best pleased to discover their home had been without an alarm for a while. Karen said she and Diane would meet him at the house at nine on Thursday evening – and she told her boyfriend of her good luck in picking up an easy hundred bucks.

Meanwhile, Kenny checked out the house, identified the basement as the best location for what he had in mind and made sure that there was a length of strong cord there. When the two girls got there, Kenny was waiting outside in his company truck. He suggested that Karen accompany him inside to turn on the lights, and he'd be back in a moment to conduct Diane inside. As he was – the moment Karen reached the basement, he wrapped the cord around her throat and strangled her with such force that she made no cry at all. He immediately returned to invite Diane inside, and throttled her with equal speed.

Neither girl was either raped or sodomized. Kenny merely masturbated on the corpses, still fully clothed as they were, before dragging them back up the stairs, and putting them in Karen's hatchback Mercury, which he then drove to a cul-de-sac less than a mile away. There he left it, walked back to the house and drove the pick-up home, disposing of the murder cord on the way.

What a hundred Los Angeles cops had failed to do in 16 months, the Bellingham police force managed in less than 24 hours. Kenny had clearly never quite understood that Angelo Buono's magical immunity depended on some deeply mundane rules: don't kill people who can easily be identified, then easily be linked to you; don't do it in a place which can quickly be identified; and always do your housekeeping.

As soon as the bodies were found – within hours – and

identified – within minutes of discovery, the Bellingham detectives were at Karen and Diane's apartment. There was a note from Diane to Karen reporting Kenny's original call. An interview with Karen's boyfriend, who might in Los Angeles have been treated as an automatic suspect, instead turned up full details of the house-sitting job. A trip to Kenny's house revealed an Aladdin's cave of obviously stolen goods – and Kenny was arrested, on the holding charge of grand larceny, on Friday, 12 January, barely hours after he had started work again.

Still in his possession was his California driver's licence: it gave both his former addresses at East Garfield and Tamarind, and the Bellingham force sent out a routine call to the LA County Sheriff's Department to check on his background. They certainly weren't thinking 'Hillside Strangler' at that moment up in Washington, but the moment their enquiry came in it was passed to Frank Salerno, who made the instant connection.

As Frank says, 'I was actually in my garage when the call came in – I had taken the weekend off, and this was the Saturday. My lieutenant asked me if I was sitting down, and I said, "No, I'm standing up: tell me what you've got – is this another one of those false leads?" and he said, "We've got a call from Bellingham, Washington. They've got an individual who's a suspect in a double murder and guess where he lived?", and I says, "Phil, I don't know: tell me."'

800 Garfield was Christina Weckler's address. 804 Garfield was Cindy Hudspeth's address. The apartment block on

Tamarind was where Kimberley Martin had been summoned. As Frank ruefully admits, 'We never had a connection like that ever: in the entire time this task force was running we never became aware that we had a suspect we could connect to three of the crimes, so I said, "I'll be right there", and I went to the office.'

There, Frank pulled the complete list of all those ever named or interviewed in the Hillside investigation. But this time, thanks to Bellingham, he had a key name: and for the first time in all those months, it became glaringly obvious that Kenneth Bianchi was mentioned no less than five times.

It was Sunday, 14 January 1978. Bob Grogan had just got back from another wild goose-chase, this time to Colorado, following a fictitious lead, when he got the long-distance call from his partner, Dudley Varney, up in Washington. The moment he heard what had taken Varney and Frank Salerno to Bellingham – two stranglings by a man who had once lived on both East Garfield and on Tamarind – he knew they were finally getting there. And when Varney told him that a search of Bianchi's house had turned up a cache of jewellery, including a ring which fitted the description of one worn by Yolanda Washington and a necklace which matched one of Kimberley Martin's, Grogan's only question was, "What about the other guy?"

Kelli Boyd, who had already convinced the detectives that she was completely unaware of what Bianchi got up to when away from home, had told them that his only friend in Los Angeles was his cousin Angelo Buono, an automobile upholsterer in Glendale. Suddenly, Grogan regretted being quite so dismissive of the German detective who had offered them the 'two Italian brothers' hypothesis.

Suddenly all those earlier clues, once so unhelpful, began to fall into place. But there were still several convoluted problems to surmount. It obviously helped when a photograph of the suspect Bianchi in the press brought forward David Wood and the story of Becky and Sabra, but Angelo Buono was admitting nothing about anything. And Kenny Bianchi, as it dawned on him that the State of Washington had enough evidence to convict him on the Bellingham murders, introduced a further massive red herring into the case.

Among his many fantasies, Kenny had frequently pretended to be qualified in psychology, and with the aid of some faked diplomas had even persuaded a genuine therapist to let him have office space at one time. Now, with his life on the line, he drew partly on his readings in the subject, and partly on his knowledge of the movie 'The Three Faces of Eve', to invent himself as the victim of a multiple-personality disorder. By his account, decent, law-abiding Kenny also played unwitting host to wicked, crude, murderous Steve. Indeed, he managed to persuade a particularly gullible forensic psychiatrist that there was certainly something to his claim – who then called in a second opinion from a colleague, Dr John Watkins, who had spent much of his career advocating the multiple-personality theory.

The cops were outraged as they witnessed Kenny's interviews with the clinicians. Salerno wrote BULLSHIT in large letters in his notebook, while Grogan said, 'I got a great idea. The judge should say to Bianchi, "Mr Bianchi, I'll tell you what I'm going to do. I'm going to let Ken off. Ken is acquitted. But Steve gets the chair."'

But there was a bonus in all this pretence. As he sought to build an insanity defence for himself, Kenny (or Steve, or Billy, a third personality Kenny produced for inspection as soon as one of his interrogators let drop a hint that most classic cases had shown more than one hidden personality) had to incriminate someone, and that was Angelo. So with every twist and turn of his own convoluted scam, he supplied more and more leads to help the police trap his cousin.

Gradually, the story began to unfold. It seemed that when the cousins lost Becky and Sabra and the income they had been generating, their first move, using the police badges, was to try to abduct a young woman off the street. But the girl they picked wasn't a whore at all – she identified herself as Catherine Lorre, daughter of the film star Peter Lorre, and Angelo had more than enough presence of mind to send her on her way with some official advice to watch where she walked.

They did eventually recruit a replacement tenant for Sabra's old room, but needed to rebuild their customer base. Another prostitute, Deborah Noble, agreed to sell them her own 'trick list', and delivered it, in company with her friend Yolanda Washington, in October 1977.

According to Noble, it was well worth a dollar a name, since these were all out-call customers, who would ring in for girls to be sent to them. When Angelo and Kenny discovered that it was nothing of the sort, and that every single name on the list expected to be able to call round to Angelo's when the fancy took them, they were outraged. They decided Deborah would be made to pay for her deceit.

But while they didn't know how to find Noble, Yolanda Washington had foolishly let drop exactly which stretch of Sunset Boulevard she normally worked. And so, on October 17, they drove out to her beat, used Angelo's badge to persuade her they were really under-cover vice cops, hand-cuffed her and threw her into the back seat of Kenny's Cadillac.

Bianchi stripped and then raped her as Angelo drove along the Hollywood Freeway, and then began to strangle her. Yolanda did resist at that point, so Angelo held her down by her legs as Kenny finished the job. They dumped her body on Forest Lawn Drive and got rid of all her clothing in a large skip behind Angelo's workshop – although larcenous Kenny couldn't resist slipping her distinctive turquoise ring into his pocket when Angelo wasn't looking.

So that's how it began. Yolanda hadn't even been respon-sible for cheating them out of $175, but she bore the brunt of their unimaginable rage. And worse, her murder seems both to have given them a taste for killing, and the sense that they could get away with it.

At any rate, within a fortnight Judy Miller became the second victim of their indiscriminate contempt for whores, and a week later, so did Lissa Kastin. Judy was picked up by the same bogus cop routine, but taken back to Angelo's to be stripped, bound, raped, sodomized and killed. And not only was she bound, but her eyes taped over with materials from the workshop, a single fragment of which was to be scrupulously collected by Frank Salerno and kept as potential evidence for all the ensuing months.

Naturally, when the police finally got their lead from Kenny's interrogations, they hoped they would be able to gather far more linking evidence from Angelo Buono's home and workshop. But if Kenny had demonstrated a laughable sloppiness in covering his Bellingham trail, his older cousin had displayed a truly obsessional concern for destroying evidence. When Grogan finally got a search warrant, and moved the police technicians into Angelo's for three whole days of exhaustive examination, using a chemical spray which is capable of lifting fingerprints up to several years old, they got a shock. They could find none: not even Buono's own.

But they did find, in the workshop, fibres which matched that tiny fleck on Judy Miller's eye: and, in the house, matches for the unique bunch of fibres on Lauren Wagner's wrist turned up in the spare bedroom – some on a chair and some on the carpet. Better still, houseproud Angelo had left one job uncompleted – although he had dumped his police badge, he had forgotten to destroy the wallet in which it had been pinned, and that turned up in a desk drawer in his office, still bearing both the pin-holes and the depressed outline of the shield.

However, Angelo denied everything. In fact, as Grogan remembers, 'He wouldn't even admit to the most obvious – I mean, there's got to be some things you admit to, things that are non-criminal, and this guy just stonewalled everything. We were purposefully asking questions that we knew were obviously true and that had no criminal consequence, and he would say, "No: I don't know anything." This guy was tough – he was stonewalling everything.'

In the circumstances, as Kenny's 'multiple personality' con steadily unravelled, it became clear it would be an uphill struggle for him to beat a conviction – but possibly just as hard to make one stick to Angelo without Kenny's testimony. So, as is rather more openly done in America than elsewhere, plea bargaining came into the equation.

The Los Angeles County District Attorney's Office sketched out the deal. If Kenny pleaded guilty to the Washington murders and some of the Hillside ones, and agreed to testify in detail against his cousin, he would get life imprisonment with the possibility of parole and serve his time in California, which was reputed among cons to be a rather easier regime than that in Washington's feared Walla Walla penitentiary – plus, of course, no longer any risk that Washington would insist on the death penalty.

So the details gradually accumulated: how Kristina Weckler, the first unquestionably respectable victim, had been picked up in the usual way, handcuffed, taken back to Angelo's, stripped, bound, subjected to a variety of sexual assaults and then had a plastic bag put over her head into which a pipe from the stove was inserted, so that she died a protracted death from asphyxiation, but only after the cousins had injected her three times with a corrosive cleaner – the two needle marks which had been noticed on her arm, and a third, on her neck, which had been missed until Kenny casually mentioned it; how the two young Mexican-American girls, chosen because the stranglers had long abandoned the pretence that it was only whores who deserved their attentions, had been all too eager to co-operate with the 'police' because they had just been shoplifting when intercepted at the Eagle Rock Plaza. Jane King – waiting for a bus on her way back from class at a Scientology centre. Lauren Wagner, whom the cousins had tried to electrocute, just to ring the changes, which is why she had those burn marks on her hands and the fibres still glued to her wrists where the flex had been taped to them. Kimberley Diane Martin, the call-girl who had been despatched, against all the rules, in response to a request from a pay-phone, had panicked at the sight of the empty apartment, but been dragged in by Bruno and Bianchi. And finally, Cindy Hudspeth, who had gone in all innocence to Angelo's Trim Shop because she needed some work on her Datsun.

The picture was filling out, the evidence falling into place, but Angelo wasn't admitting anything and Kenny still had several more bizarre shots in his locker. Sure, he'd apparently assented to a plea bargain and been found out in his first shot at an insanity defence, but he now began changing his stories and, although he had been transferred from Washington to California, still reckoned he could find a way out.

What was truly astonishing, even for those accustomed to

Kenny Bianchi's breathtaking sociopathy, was that he found – from inside jail – a willing accomplice in his wildest scheme of all. Veronica Compton was an aspiring writer, working on a play about a serial killer to be called 'The Mutilated Cutter.' Quite why the prison authorities in any jurisdiction would allow such a woman to start a correspondence with a known serial killer, followed by unmonitored phone calls, and finally visits, most of us would find difficult to fathom, but that's what happened. Veronica decided she was in love with Bianchi, and wanted to spend her life with him – but, naturally, on the outside. How could that be achieved ? Easy, said Kenny: all she needed to do was go up to Bellingham, armed with a length of cord and a sample of Kenny's sperm, and murder some other girl. Kenny would have a perfect alibi, plus good cause for suggesting that the real Bellingham strangler was still at large and that he, Kenny, was the victim of a miscarriage of justice.

At this point, it's necessary to assure the reader that there is no doubt whatsoever that that was the plan, and that Veronica Compton found it perfectly rational, and just the kind of thing any decent woman would do to help her proposed lover. Fortunately, on arrival in Bellingham with her cord and smuggled condom of Bianchi's semen (pre-DNA, it would establish only that the same man was responsible, NOT that it had to be Kenny), Veronica fortified herself with so much cocaine and booze that her chosen victim was easily able to fight her off. So back Veronica flew to San Francisco, where she created such a disturbance at the airport that her photograph was taken, and swiftly found to match the description given by the woman she had tried to strangle. Kenny's scheme hadn't got him out of jail, but instead got Veronica in. What's more, she got no choice but to serve her sentence in Washington.

Still, the protracted battle to make sure Angelo did time was winding endlessly on. He had finally been arrested on 22 October 1979, a little over two years after Yolanda Washington had been killed. The preliminary hearing in Municipal Court, to establish that there was a case to answer, took ten months from May 1980.

The wheels of Californian justice certainly turn slowly, but at last Angelo Buono was sent for trial. The judge assigned to the case was Ronald M.George, subsequently to become Chief Justice of California, but then a Judge of the Superior Court. The first hurdle to be negotiated was a minor blizzard of procedural motions, largely based on the bewildering variety of scams, pretences and conflicting stories which had sprung from Kenneth Bianchi. But once that was complete, the man in charge of the prosecution, District Attorney Roger Kelly, had yet another astonishing twist of his own to offer. Convinced that it would be hard to get a conviction depending on the evidence of Bianchi, and, indeed, of Beulah Stofer, he made a motion to dismiss the charges against Buono completely.

Bob Grogan and Frank Salerno were incandescent with rage. Grogan's view of Kelly, 20 years on, still reflects that: 'Roger Kelly? God rest his soul, he's dead now, but I hated the bastard. He was a good prosecutor as long as he had a signed confession and a smoking gun, but if it required work, Roger Kelly was as worthless as tits on a bull. I wanted to go over and shoot Roger Kelly. I mean, we were, like, defeated here; here's all this work, this is a couple of years, and all this shit has gone down the tubes because of somebody's ego.'

Now it's fairly standard practice that if the prosecution, as well as the defence, makes a motion to dismiss, the judge just accepts it. But Judge George didn't feel, as he now says, that 'I should act as a rubber stamp either for the prosecution or the defence, but rather, I should make independent determination whether dismissal would be in the interests of justice.' To Kelly's surprise, therefore, he merely adjourned the case for a week and said he would then give his ruling.

It was a slim hope: so while the defence team celebrated, Grogan and Salerno merely drowned their sorrows.

On Tuesday, 21 July, the courtroom was full, Buono and his lawyers in far more optimistic spirits than Grogan, Salerno and their colleagues. But slowly, as Judge George detailed his reasonings and approached his conclusion – he had written some 36 pages – the mood began to change. And at the point at which he declared: 'This court would be abdicating the responsibility of its office were it to permit the District Attorney to abort this massive and costly three-and-a-half-year investigation', Grogan recalls: 'It was like my whole lightbulb went on. This was the happiest day of my life and I ran down and bought a bottle of champagne and I came back to the courthouse and I went up to Ron George's chambers and walked in, and Ron says, "I can't do that" – and I says, "I know you can't, but do you mind standing there watching me?". And I said, "Thanks for allowing the system to work, Your Honour: you're a judge with balls."'

The immediate consequence of this almost unprecedented decision was that the District Attorney was ordered to proceed, and plainly could not do so with any remaining credibility, so the prosecution was turned over to the Attorney General's office. In other words, the detectives had to brief an entirely new set of lawyers in a case where the preliminary hearing alone had generated several thousand pages of transcripts and motions, and there were about 400 witnesses to be called.

Grogan didn't underestimate the challenge facing the new prosecutors, Roger Boren and Michael Nash. 'Can you imagine, coming in cold on a case like that – I mean cold turkey? Here's two guys who only know what they've been reading in the papers.' And Boren, later to become a Presiding Justice of the California Court of Appeal, still recalls being brought 'many, many boxes – there were over 10,000 files generated' and that 'there weren't many mornings that I didn't wake up to think, "You know, if we don't do a good job there's going to be a lot of tax-payers' money wasted."'

The new team was granted a two-month continuance to master its massive brief, and finally, on 16 November 1981, the process of jury selection began, four years after that terrible Thanksgiving week when five bodies were discovered strewn on Californian hillsides. Yet so determinedly obstructive were the defence that it was to be a further three and a half months before the trial proper could begin – in the

Spring of 1982, with the prospect of at least another year in court. In fact, it was to last two years – the longest criminal trial in Californian history.

However, the trail which began with Yolanda Washington in October 1977 finally wound to its conclusion in October 1983, when the jury was sent off to deliberate its verdicts. That, too, was to take some time (there were, after all, more than 50,000 pages of transcripts by that time), and it was not until 9 January 1984, Buono having been found guilty of all the murders save that of Yolanda, that Judge George was able to pronounce formal sentence: he would have been more than happy to sentence Buono to death, but the jury, probably because they knew that Bianchi had negotiated his way out of the ultimate penalty, had tied his hands. Their conclusion was that Buono, too, should be imprisoned, not executed.

As George said 'I would not have the slightest reluctance to impose the death penalty in this case were it within my power to do so. If ever there was a case where the death penalty is appropriate, this is that case. Angelo Buono and Kenneth Bianchi slowly squeezed out of their victims their last breath of air, and their promise of a future life. And all for what ? The momentary sadistic thrill of enjoying a brief, perverted sexual satisfaction and the venting of their hatred for women.'

All he could do to Buono was declare that he 'should never see the outside of prison walls.' But in Bianchi's case, there was one small chink of opportunity for the judge to express his anger. Ronald George ruled that Kenny had made a mockery of his plea bargain to give full and truthful testimony – so he sent him back to Walla Walla to serve out his life term, rather than granting him the allegedly easier conditions of the California system.

And as Bob Grogan said, 'That was the best part of the whole verdict, sending that asshole back to the State of Washington.' Next best was that Angelo Buono, in Grogan's words, 'was a guy that loves his women, and he ain't gonna have any any more.'

Nor, one must assume, did he. Prison guards checking his cell on the morning of 21 September 2002, found Angelo Buono dead of a heart attack. An autopsy revealed that the 67-year-old had suffered from coronary artery disease, and died in his sleep.

DAVID CARPENTER –
THE TRAILSIDE KILLER

The Trailside Murders in the vast forests around San Francisco began in August 1979, and no arrest was made until May 1981. For that matter, the trials wound on until 1988, and the killer has now been staving off execution for 14 years, becoming comfortably the oldest resident on Death Row.

Stark numbers like that feature quite a lot in this case. One: the killer had more than 200,000 acres of wilderness to use as his stalking-ground. Two: at one stage the various investigating forces had a list of more than 4,000 suspects. Three: the trails through the glorious Golden Gate scenery attract one-and-a-half million people (suspects? potential victims?) every year. And four: while nobody will ever know how many victims the Trailside Killer claimed, the FBI's estimate is 'over 20.'

And the awful tragedy is that the murderer might have

been caught much earlier but for two critical mistakes in the sheriff's office of Marin County. First, they became fixated by a photofit of a suspect who wasn't the killer at all – and second, they jumped to an entirely erroneous conclusion about a man whose long criminal record should have put him high on their lists from the very start.

Of course, as with any serial murderer, nobody can be expected to leap to the conclusion that there's one at large just on the evidence of the first victim, and police professionals all over the world will sympathize with Marin County, whose first instinct on the discovery of Edda Kane's body on Mount Tamalpais was, as retired Detective Sergeant Rich Keaton of the Sheriff's Office admits, 'to look at anybody and everybody as a possible suspect, but her husband was high on our radar for a while.'

Statistically, they were perfectly justified – so long as Edda was the only victim on the woodland trails, the chances were that she had been killed by someone she knew. Once others begin to turn up, however, grimmer suspicions start to occur. Still, let's begin with Edda.

Edda Kane was 44 years old, and had a senior job with the Bank of America. She and her husband John, almost 20 years older and seemingly less successful, had moved some ten years earlier from North Hollywood to Mill Valley, one of the 13 small cities in Marin County. 11 of the cities cluster round the dominating Mount Tamalpais, each one of which has its own separate police force. Not quite as bad as it seems – most contract out their serious criminal investigations to the

County Sheriff's Office – but further complicated by the fact that the Golden Gate National Park Reserve is a Federal, not a California, State Park and thus technically subject to the jurisdiction of the Park Rangers, and, in extreme circumstances, of the FBI. Law enforcement under those conditions can be bureaucratically cumbersome.

On Sunday, 19 August 1979, Edda, a keen member of a hiking club called the Nature Friends Tourists, was anxious to get out on to the neighbouring mountain. John's arthritis was giving him pain, so he was unwilling to tackle the four-hour trek. Edda rang a fellow-member of the club, but got no reply. In the circumstances (and at that time, Mount Tamalpais enjoyed an almost mystical reputation as a place of peace in which no harm had ever come to anyone) Edda happily went off alone. So, then, might any of her fellow-citizens, since Marin County, the fifth-richest in the whole of California, combined ecological enthusiasm with a touching confidence in human nature.

Or, as Rich Keaton puts it, 'This county has a great love for the environment: we have people here that are very, very active in saving the open space, and saving the trees, and stopping building projects because of a titmouse or a lizard: vehement about protecting the trails and the mountains, nature-lovers, hot-tubbers, and it was unheard-of to have a firearm in the Parks. They really didn't want the Rangers wearing guns – they knew the need for it, but it seemed to me as I got more educated that this was like committing a crime in church: it was a violation of sanctity.'

And as a matter of fact, for all his cynicism, Rich Keaton has his own rather sheepish Marin County admission to make. 'There are stories told about when emergencies occurred and I had to go find a gun, because I didn't carry one with me most of the time. It was in the trunk of my car unless I needed it.'

He certainly didn't know he might need it when his convivial night out with police colleagues at a local bar was interrupted by a phone call telling him to respond to a report of a dead body on the mountain. When Edda had failed to return home the previous evening, John Kane had reported her missing. A night search had been conducted, without success, but the following morning suspicions grew stronger when her car was found, still parked at the foot of the trails. Eventually, Edda's body had been found, face-down in a kneeling position, with the entry wound of a large-calibre bullet visible in the back of her head. She was naked except for a single sock.

Keaton drove up in the gathering darkness, by no means certain of where he was going. 'I'm a city boy', he says, 'and I was in coat and tie, wing-tipped shoes, driving my Cadillac, which my wife used to call my "pimp-mobile", and I didn't know where the hell I was. They finally sent Rangers down to a parking lot to meet me, so that I could go to the crime scene and observe. It was probably 10.30 at night before I got there, and I remember it was God-awful dark. I had a five-cell flashlight and it was useless. I mean, you could see, but this rocky terrain – narrow footpaths – when your light was off, it was as if you were inside a box; you couldn't see anything.'

The milling crowd of Rangers, detectives and employees of the coroner's office took photographs as best they could, and taped off the scene ready for the following morning. One deputy slept overnight at the scene, although one might suspect he didn't shut his eyes for long.

The normal routine swung into action. The autopsy showed that Edda had actually been shot twice, at very close quarters since both bullets had entered her skull in the same place, and the weapon was a .44 calibre. On a fine summer's day there had been plenty of other hikers scattered around the mountain, and as many as possible (more than 500, in fact – just an indication of the amount of leg-work the case was to involve) were traced to be asked if they had seen anything suspicious. The result was a couple of artist's impressions of men who had, one way or another, caught the attention of fellow-hikers: a hooded man and a blond young man.

It can't be said that much progress was being made. Indeed, there was still no reason to believe that the killer would strike again, although poor John Kane had been removed from the suspect lists and left to nurse his grief over a deskful of photographs of Edda and an ever-present bottle. In fact, only hindsight now suggests that the Trailside killer was at work when a 23-year-old jogger, Mary Frances Bennett, was viciously stabbed to death in Lincoln Park, near San Francisco, on Sunday, 21 October 1979. Hindsight becomes more persuasive when it turns out that the man who was eventually to be convicted of a string of other park land killings reported to the emergency department of Marin

General Hospital that same evening with multiple lacera-
tions on his hands. He told the doctor that he had been bitten
by a dog while out hiking.

Hindsight, but no court conviction, also suggests that the
same man murdered Barbara Schwarz on the slopes of
Mount Tamalpais on Saturday, 8 March 1980. When a location has been entirely free of violent crime for untold
generations, and two particularly vicious murders occur
there within a few months, both of lone women hikers, it does
give pause for thought. Keaton wasn't himself directly
involved in the Schwarz killing – not least because she, like
Mary Frances Bennett, was stabbed, not shot as Edda Kane
had been. Nevertheless, others who had been on the mountain that Saturday gave descriptions of an apparently
agitated young male hiker, and, as Keaton recollects,
'someone in the office made a quantum leap, that we were
going to go ahead and use this composite as a possible lead.
So it went all over the world that we were looking for a young
male with a backpack and thick hair.'

Indeed, when two further witnesses came forward they
were shown the composite, and when they said that the man
they had seen didn't look like it at all, but rather more like
an accountant, the officers lost interest.

There were also two pieces of physical evidence. Near
Barbara's body was a pair of black-framed glasses. Both their
style and the serial number on the side-piece identified them
as the kind issued in prisons. Marin County circularized both
prisons and optometrists with the prescription, but nobody

could find a match in their records, perhaps because the Sheriff's Office told them they were looking for a young man – the subject of the composite – and because quite a few optometrists never even got the flyer.

Even worse, when two young students stumbled across a blood-stained knife on the trail they attracted the attention of a TV crew, who promptly picked it up to show it to the camera, effectively ruining any hope of fingerprints, which again might have been circularized round the police forces and the prisons in search of a match.

But California's prison records had already contributed their own red herring to the investigation. Checks had been made to see if any inmates with records of sexual violence had been recently discharged or paroled. One whose previous form certainly fitted had been – but only to the federal authorities, to complete a sentence with them. Marin County Sheriff's Office assumed that ruled him out – without establishing that the federal authorities were operating a release-on-licence scheme to ease offenders back into the community.

So while all efforts were being concentrated on finding a young man with thick, dark hair, a middle-aged man who had already been balding fast when first imprisoned for a violent assault and attempted rape in 1960 was out on federal parole, taking a computer printing course.

David Carpenter had been born in 1930 to very strict parents, and was generally remembered by schoolmates, and later colleagues in the Merchant Marine (he had been a purser – as close as ships get to having an accountant on board) and the US Coastguard as having a pronounced stutter, and being aggressive in his dealings with women.

Whereas Hillside Strangler Angelo Buono had learnt from the Caryl Chessman case that a rapist should never leave a living witness to his crimes, David Carpenter had finally learnt that lesson from his own bitter experience. After serving nine years of a 14-year sentence for the attack in 1960, he was paroled from federal prison (the attack had taken place in the grounds of a military base) and soon went on a spree of rapes, assaults and abductions. All his victims lived to testify against him, in January 1970. For those, he received sentences of five years to life in the California correction system. If and when he was paroled, he would then be handed back to the federal authorities for violation of his earlier parole.

Carpenter, balding, bespectacled, stuttering – and bright, with a prison-tested IQ of 125 – was a model inmate. Marin County District Attorney John Posey says of him: 'Throughout the years, he had this uncanny ability to fool a lot of people. He was disarming in his approach; he was very good at conning expert witnesses.' This is, of course, the smart way to get parole, to keep a probation officer happy and, as one detective later said, 'slip between the cracks of the system'.

And so it came about that, more than a year after the murder of Edda Kane, the investigators remained fixated on the unknown young man with ample hair, and unaware that David Carpenter had long since left his federal cell for virtually total freedom under the light supervision of a probation officer: was, indeed, back living with his parents, earning money, driving a car, dealing in marijuana and dreaming up get-rich-quick schemes involving pornographic key-rings.

Monday, 13 October 1980 was the Columbus Day holiday. Annie Alderson, aged 26, left her parents' home in the afternoon to visit her 90-year-old grandmother in the East Bay area. She did not return. On the following day, she was reported missing, and her car was found parked at the entrance to the trails on Mount Tamalpais. It would have been perfectly in character for her to stop off there to meditate for a while, and indeed a witness recollected seeing her there in the early evening, just by the open-air amphitheatre. To get there, she must have passed one of the warning notices that by now counselled visitors, particularly lone women, to be on their guard.

The moment the news reached the Sheriff's Office – missing person, lone young woman, car still in the car park for the mountain forest – as Keaton says, 'We're all going. "Jesus, bet we've got another victim", and at that point too investigators started looking at each other wondering, "Could it be a Ranger? Could it be a maintenance person? Could it be someone working for the Park, or a fireman, somebody who is up there and has reason to be up there?"'

That unsettling thought was reinforced when one long-serving Ranger announcing that he knew 'the spots where the kids go, either to have a booze party or to make out, have a little sexual orgy', went off to search them, and found Annie's body. As Keaton admits, one colleague immediately said,

'We've got to look at him: he may be a suspect', although his
own view, having known the man all his life, was that 'killing
a girl would not be his forte – he'd rather make love to them.'

Nevertheless, the discovery was shocking. Annie was
totally dressed, had been shot in the head and turned over
after the first shot to be given a coup de grace. The autopsy
reports revealed that she had been raped, and strongly
suggested that she had been first stripped and then told to
get dressed again before being shot through the eye.

Forest crime scenes, however quickly the investigators
arrive, have their special difficulties. As Keaton says, 'You
know, when you come up the side of a mountain, there isn't
anything there but the animals, the deer and raccoons, and
you are looking for physical evidence, but it's practically
impossible to find – you are walking on leaves, and if you don't
find it right away, in hours or days, with the wind and the rain
and animals pulling body parts, you're not really working
with a lot. In this particular case we were lucky, because he
had a gun and bullets, and we had a calibre to go by, but something that was never reported or documented in any trial is
that I went back sometime afterwards, and round where
Annie was shot I found some string and an empty 35mm film
canister in adjacent bushes. We believe that there were photographs taken at that scene: we can't prove it, but there were
marks that looked like tripod marks on the turf. My gut
feeling was that we had got somebody taking home trophies.'

One thing was beginning to fall into place, however. The
murders were taking place on weekends or holidays – which

suggested that the killer was in a regular job. And at this junc-
ture, Marin County turned to the newly-established skills of
the criminal profilers. Not all the seasoned investigators took it
seriously – Keaton remembers that many colleagues 'thought it
was voodoo or witchcraft, probably one step removed from the
psychics' – but an FBI special agent, John Douglas, was
brought in to make his own assessment. He made it clear that
he only wanted the hard evidence, crime-scene photographs,
bald facts, autopsy reports, and not any theories or suspicions
the Sheriff's officers had in mind. Then, to Keaton's surprise,
'He locked himself into a hotel right across the freeway from
the Hall of Justice, got in there on a Friday, and stayed there
incommunicado for almost the whole weekend. Monday
morning he came in to give us a briefing, and it was going to be
a one-bite-of-the-apple, top secret -type thing: the copies were
numbered and had to be signed for, and mustn't be copied. '

Frankly, it wasn't much help. Not only did Douglas rein-
force the notion that the perpetrator was a young white male
(25 to 35), but it couldn't have surprised anyone when he
suggested that he would be a loner, probably have a criminal
record and hang out in bars. Rather like the composite, it
helped some detectives to close their minds to anything
which didn't fall exactly into place, and thus to ignore any
potential lead which seemed off-line. As Keaton says, 'How
did we know it wasn't a black guy – an old man – a woman?
If you're going to get so myopic as to discontinue reviewing
other candidate suspects because of the profile, we might just
as well can the whole system.'

And there was always the worrying thought that there might be more than one killer: a .44 gun in one case, knives in two others and now, with Alderson, a .38 gun. Similar victims, similar locations, but different weapons – which would make it all the harder to prove that any eventual defendant could be linked to every case.

The State of California does maintain a register of sexual offenders – in 1980 there were an amazing 58,000 names on it – but however often the investigators ran it through their computer, it was never going to come up with David Carpenter's name. As far as California was concerned, he was still in prison, and as far as the federal officials were concerned, it wasn't their business to register him when they let him out. In any case, a study in 1977 had revealed that 94 per cent of all California police forces had failed to prosecute a single sex offender for failing to register or to notify the police of a change of address. To all intents and purposes, it was – perhaps still is – a voluntary system.

Then, suddenly, Marin County got not just two more murders but a brand-new suspect, for whom they had both a name and a photograph. What's more, it was a young man with a pony-tail and a long history of mental disturbance. When Sheriff's officers drove out to the McDermand family home on the slopes of Tamalpais in response to calls from worried neighbours who had not seen either Mrs McDermand or either of her two sons for two days – since some of them believed they had heard a volley of gunfire from the decrepit shack – they discovered the mother and her son Edwin dead and Edwin's brother Mark missing. The time of the killings was established as late at night on Monday, 13 October – just a few hours after Annie Alderson had died.

Understandably, that made Mark not only the prime suspect for those killings, but for the string of Trailside murders. It seemed to be most unlikely that an area which had for so long enjoyed a reputation for tranquility and order should suddenly turn out to harbour two quite separate multiple killers. Besides, Mark did bear an apparent likeness to the precious composite, and in one photograph was wearing glasses very like those found at the Schwarz crime scene. Accordingly, the entire investigation now concentrated on finding Mark and his 11-year-old yellow Chevrolet. No one wondered why a killer who had previously left little or no traceable evidence should actually have pinned a note on the wall of his house for the detectives to find (signed 'Mr Hate') and then contacted both journalists and investigators by letter and telephone while on the run.

It took 11 days before Mark rang the Marin County Sheriff's Office and effectively invited them to come and arrest him at a local pancake house. Ballistics were already indicating that the gun used to kill his mother and brother certainly wasn't one of those used in the Trailside killings, and inside a month it became all too plain that whatever else he had done, Mark McDermand hadn't committed them – because he was very definitely in jail when the Trailside killer struck again.

This time, the location was the Point Reyes National

Seashore Park, a wooded peninsula which juts into the Pacific north of San Francisco. It has no fewer than 145 miles of wilderness trails. On Friday, 28 November 1980 (the day after the Thanksgiving holiday), three young women decided to hike one of those trails. Diane O'Connell, Nancy Dagle and Sharon Raymond were friends, all in their early 20s but of different levels of fitness, and quite soon they agreed it was easier if each took her own pace – ending up spread over a hundred yards or more of the winding forest path, with Sharon in the lead, Diane next and Nancy bringing up the rear. There were plenty of other hikers in the Park that day but, because of the thick woodland, there remained a sense of privacy, and it was always with a sense of surprise that hikers rounded a corner and suddenly saw somebody else on their particular trail. Sharon came upon one young man who rather frightened her – she wasn't sure if he was merely urinating in a bush or exposing himself – which was to prove yet another handicap to the investigation since he, whoever he was and whatever he had in mind, wasn't the Trailside Killer, but did correspond to the obsessional composite.

Another hiker, a university worker, was to report that the most suspicious person she had seen on the trail that day was about 50, wearing glasses, his head covered by a baseball cap, with an angry expression, and carrying a bag, not a pack.

Sharon, leading the way down the track, had exchanged greetings with yet another woman hiker on her way up – whose name was to emerge as Shauna May. At the end of the descending path, Sharon stopped to await her friends. To her

surprise, it wasn't Diane but Nancy who turned up next –
who was surprised herself not to find Diane there, since she
certainly hadn't overtaken her. Nor had she seen anything of
Shauna May. The two women waited awhile, then retraced
their steps up the last stretch of path, and finally reported
Diane's mysterious disappearance to the Park Rangers in the
early evening. Very shortly afterwards, a friend of Shauna
May called in to report her missing, too. Although a search
was begun immediately, the darkness and the drifting sea-
fog forced them to call it off until the following morning.

The next day, as teams of Rangers and volunteers began to
work their way through the 70,000 acres of the park, a call
went out for help to the Coastguard, the Highway Patrol and
Marin County Sheriff's Office. To Rich Keaton and his
colleagues, any reports of missing persons in parkland now
automatically set the alarm bells ringing, and he and his
partner set off once more into the unknown because, as Rich
admits, 'If it didn't have paved streets and running water, I
wasn't about to be there.'

On their way, the two investigators rather hoped that their
workload wasn't about to be increased – Keaton's exact
words were, 'Hey, this is a Federal park, thank fuck: this is
FBI – the big boys are coming in now.' Things aren't that
simple. As the search continued, a volunteer found two
bodies – but they weren't two recently-slain women, but a
man and a woman who had been dead for quite a time.
Subsequently, not very far from that site, searchers found the
bodies of Diane and Shauna. Then the FBI told the sheriff

that although they would of course be happy to handle the case, they wouldn't insist if he didn't think it necessary.

So much for Keaton's optimism. While he and his partner sat in the woods, clutching their rapidly-fading flashlights and waiting to be relieved by the FBI and the Coroner's men, the politically-ambitious Sheriff was making it clear that his department could, and would, handle the case. When the news was broken to Keaton, still squatting out at the crime scene, he protested – 'I said, "This is Federal parkland; there's four bodies in it; we're not equipped to handle this; we don't have the resources"' – but to no avail.

'I was so pissed', he remembers, 'because while I was sitting there five hours I could have used that time to start my collection of each and every item of clothing, and all we did was sit there and keep a light on while the politics was going on. I mean, the best investigative agency in the nation could take it, and they aren't going to.'

The unexpected bodies were identified as Cindy Moreland and Rick Stowers. They had been newly-engaged when they disappeared on 11 October 1980, and Rick, a Coastguard, had just been posted to Point Reyes. Pathologists established, despite the almost skeletal condition of the remains, that both had been shot and that in Rick's case, at least, the weapon was the one which had killed Annie Alderson, Diane O'Connell and Shauna May. Sperm samples from Annie, Diane and Shauna also matched. There was no longer much doubt that the Trailside murders were connected, but still no genuine lead to the murderer himself.

What was clear was that he went about his business well equipped. Slowly, the evidence was building up that he identified, stalked and laid in wait for his chosen victims, and carried not only a weapon but wire to bind their wrists. And there was a growing suspicion that he might now be growing so confident that he had deliberately killed his latest victims a mere 200 yards from Rick and Cindy, so that their previously-undiscovered murders would be added to his tally.

Understandably, the Sheriff of Marin County's confidence was seeping away. He had an election to fight in 1982, and posters had started to appear which said 'Dump Howenstein. Make Marin Safe Again.' When the election came, the very political Sheriff who had so infuriated Keaton was indeed dumped – and Keaton's partner, Chuck Prandi, got the job. And although Howenstein had grandstanded the FBI, there was nothing he could do to ease out the detectives from Daly City who were involved because of Point Reyes – or those from San José, who were about to become involved. Rather later than some might have done, he decided to plough more money and manpower into the investigation – so that Lieutenant Don Besse, who had been off sick for a while in the Fall of 1980, returned to work to discover that his department of 14 had suddenly become one of 32, and that the Sheriff had finally gone on the record admitting there was a serial killer at large.

One obvious problem in the pursuit of serial killers who choose strangers for their victims and exploit wilderness areas is that not every one of their crimes is necessarily discovered as it happens. That certainly applied to Ivan

Milat, Aileen Wournos – and David Carpenter. So, no new bodies having turned up, and given that rather a lot of people go missing for their own good reasons and can't automatically be assumed to have been murdered just because they don't come home one night or stop turning up for work, the investigators had no knowledge of any further Trailside killings for several months. Besse's detective force shrank back by mid-March 1981 to even less than it had been the previous September, and the Sheriff unveiled a portentous 'homicide investigation decision model', based on file-cards, which was fine for putting information in but a disaster for getting it out.

Still, system, hunch or experience can all flag up the same recognition signal. And when Marin County heard that there had been a murder away to the south in the Henry Cowell Redwood State Park near Santa Cruz, their regret that yet another young woman hiker had been killed was offset by the news that her companion had survived, and had a description of the assailant. As Keaton says, 'We had our prayers answered – there was a witness who was alive and able to identify the shooter.'

The victim was Ellen Hansen. Her boyfriend was Steven Haertle. They'd gone to the park for the weekend of 28–29 March 1981, camped there for the Saturday night and on Sunday afternoon strolled the trail to and from Cathedral Grove, a ring of trees growing from a single base. There they had encountered a man whom Keaton recalls Steve describing as 'wearing a God-awful drinking jacket-type attire with emblems on it, and a baseball cap' who showed them a gun and told them he wouldn't hurt them, but he wanted to rape Ellen.

Ellen resisted. The man shot her three times, and then Steve. One bullet hit Steve in the neck, and another missed. As Keaton says, 'There were only five bullets in the type of gun he was carrying, otherwise there is no doubt that Steve would be dead also, but with the girl lying dead in a pool of blood, the young man gets up, and he starts running for help, and the murderer goes in the other direction.'

Steve's description tallied with those of other witnesses who'd encountered a middle-aged man in a bright yellow jacket at the nearby observation platform. What's more, his flight had been witnessed, right to the point where he got into his car in the parking lot, and there was therefore a partial description of the car as well.

Suddenly, the composite which had dogged and diverted the entire case had to be questioned. Now every law agency in California was being told Marin County was looking for an older white male, 45 to 55, balding, with crooked yellow teeth and glasses. Keaton describes the feeling in his office: 'Where in the hell was the 25- to 35-year-old man – the lone hiker? I mean, profiles and psychologists – well, who in the hell put out that goddam composite in the first place?'

The new flyer produced some responses, one of them from a woman who had harboured an almost obsessive loathing for a ship's officer whom she felt had tried to make improper advances to her teenage daughter on a voyage more than 25 years earlier. The officer, the purser on a passenger-carrying freighter taking the woman and her children from San Francisco to join her husband in Japan, was called David Carpenter. He had a stammer; and his attentions to her daughter had made her so worried that she had complained several times to the captain. What's more, she'd later read of his convictions for assault; and she said that the latest flyer looked just as she imagined he would now look.

It wasn't the strongest lead you could get, but it put into the system a name which was about to crop up again. San José police had a Missing Persons inquiry under way (the city is well south of San Francisco, and east of Santa Cruz) following the disappearance of a young woman called Heather Scaggs. She'd been having problems with her old car, a Volkswagen, and a workmate had told her he knew someone who could sell her a replacement at a good price. The workmate was an older man called David Carpenter.

The detective investigating Heather's disappearance was Walt Robinson, who explains how the inquiry proceeded. 'We had a young lady who could not be accounted for. Her disappearance was extremely unusual, based on her personal habits, and her Mom was very adamant that something was wrong. We started with Heather's boyfriend – he was quite concerned because he told us that Heather's car had broken down and that a co-worker had a lead on where she could get another. She had told both her Mom and her boyfriend that she was concerned about going to visit with this man – she expressed concern that if she did not get home by 6 pm her Mom should call the police. Well, of course, that sent up red flags to her mother, and she begged Heather not to go on the trip, but Heather was confident she could take care of herself, and said not to worry, she was fairly certain everything would be OK.'

Hindsight tells us that Carpenter had made his cardinal mistake: just as Kenneth Bianchi did, he had lost sight of how he had been getting away with his crimes so far – that his victims had been total strangers to him, not people he knew, who knew his name and might have talked to family and friends about him. To have left a witness alive, Steve Haertle, was bad enough: to have abducted a workmate who was known to be nervous of him suggests he had completely lost control.

Robinson's next move was to go with his partner, Ken Womack, to the print shop where Heather worked. Womack had just read the circular from Santa Cruz about the shooting of Ellen Hansen and Steve Haertle, which mentioned the car in which the assailant had been seen to escape. When they got to the print shop, says Robinson, 'we scanned the car park looking for a white Lincoln Continental that Heather's boyfriend thought he had seen her getting into on the day of her disappearance, and although we didn't see that, we did see an old, dusty red, foreign car, very similar to the description of the one seen leaving Cowell State Park.'

The two men went over to take a closer look. The flyer mentioned that the tail-pipe of the suspected killer's car was bent. So was this one. Next, Walt remembers, 'it clicked through my mind that Heather's Mom had told us Heather

had a habit of dropping Kleenex tissues wherever she went –
and I saw these tissues on the floorboards and the seat on the
passenger side. It sent a chill down my spine for a moment,
thinking we were getting close to something here, and maybe
Heather is not well.'

Having discovered that Carpenter was working at the shop
while still on early release from prison, the San José detectives let Santa Cruz know of their suspicions and decided
they should contact Carpenter's probation officer in San
Francisco, Richard Wood, and ask him to set up a meeting
with his client. 'Our game plan', says Walt, 'was just to deter-
mine what had happened to Heather from his perspective: it
was common knowledge that he had an appointment with
Heather, and now we wanted to hear what he had to say, and
where he was if he hadn't met her that day.'

The meeting took place after lunch on Friday, 8 May. The
first surprise was that Carpenter had grown a beard; second,
that he wasn't wearing glasses; and third, that he had a stuttering problem 'so severe', remembers Walt, 'that it made me
turn away: I couldn't look when he went into a contortion in
answering the first question.' But there was more to come.
When he did get out his answer, Carpenter said, 'I want to
help you guys as much as I can. I just hope that she hasn't
been raped or killed', a rather surprising response to what
was still only a possible missing person inquiry. But then, to
put him at his ease, the detectives asked him about his
personal life and interests, which turned out to include the
ballet. By pure coincidence, this also happened to be an

interest of Robinson's. What happened next amazed not just
the investigators but also Richard Wood. As Walt remembers,
'The startling thing about this was that Carpenter had
stopped stuttering from the moment we started on the ballet.
He was talking as clearly as I am.'

They were by now highly aware that they probably had the
person responsible for Heather's disappearance, and that if
he was also responsible for the Cowell Park murder it would
lead on to Marin County's homicides. Robinson and Womack
were increasingly anxious that the weekend was almost on
them, and 'this man was going to be walking free until we
could mobilize the other agencies to get this guy into custody.
We couldn't arrest him, because frankly it's not a crime to be
a missing person, and though we believed from his responses
that he was being deceitful and dishonest with us, we didn't
have a crime: we didn't have a body.' What they did have,
however, was a close look through Wood's file on Carpenter
after he'd left the meeting. From it, they discovered that
while he had been in prison one of his correspondents had
been a woman called Molly Purnell, with whom he had been
discussing some kind of investment scheme. When the two
men got back to San José, Womack began ringing colleagues
in Santa Cruz and Marin County, while Robinson followed a
hunch about Molly Purnell. The ballistics reports on the
various killings had suggested the most likely weapons were,
says Walt, 'a Taurus .38 pistol, a Rossi or an Astra, and
perhaps a .22 calibre also. I ran Molly Purnell's name
through the automated firearm licence system of the State of

California and I got a hit on two guns – one a Taurus .38 calibre, and the other a .22 calibre.'

The two detectives also put out an emergency call to the FBI and asked for a surveillance team to be put on Carpenter. By just after 7 pm on that Friday evening, they were in place, just in time for Carpenter to emerge from his house and drive away – losing the tail even though he had no idea there was one. His preoccupation, it became plain, was to get rid of the pistol he still had by dropping it off on a small-time robber of his acquaintance, Shane Williams, who had expressed interest in acquiring a weapon to use in the bank hold-ups by which he financed his wayward lifestyle.

(It was to take 11 more months before Shane Williams, back again in prison, agreed to cut a deal to tell the prosecution where that weapon was: quite an embarrassment, since the Williams apartment had been searched for it within days of Robinson's interview with Carpenter and the gun was not found, for the bizarre reason that the officers involved didn't bother to open a bag, in full view, where it happened to have been put).

Carpenter was being watched, but before making an arrest all those involved had to pool their information and agree that they had a case. The agencies involved were Marin County, Santa Cruz, San José, Daly City (who had a missing person who fitted the pattern), San Francisco and not only the FBI but also the Federal Bureau of Alcohol, Tobacco and Firearms. Although they held their first meeting in San José and the strongest evidence was held by Santa Cruz, the joint task force was put in the charge of Don Besse of Marin County. There was undoubtedly resentment about that – Marin County hadn't covered itself in glory to date, and Besse hadn't even handled their cases from the start. Nevertheless, what united all of them was that same premonition which had gripped Walt Robinson – if they didn't move fast, Carpenter might kill again. Rich Keaton recalls working for 36 hours at a stretch as the different agencies assembled enough evidence to convince not just their district attorneys, but the judge who would have to grant search and arrest warrants. Inside a week, they felt they had, and it was agreed that the arrest would be made early in the morning of Friday, 15 May, just as Carpenter left his parents' house. Once again, there were agency and personal vanities to be balanced, and the final decision was that while a whole range of premises known to have been visited by Carpenter were searched by their local agencies, the actual pinch would be made by Stoney Brook from Santa Cruz and Rich Keaton from Marin County. They didn't get on all that well – Brook claimed Keaton looked like 'a used car salesman', while Keaton plainly felt Brook was a little stiff-necked – but they both knew, as Rich says, 'we were not going to jeopardize anything: this was too good a case.'

In fact, they planned to intercept Carpenter and imply that they were still just looking for witnesses, but as they were agreeing their script in the street outside, the FBI men in their surveillance truck warned them that the suspect was on his way out. All their planned subtleties turned out to be pointless in any case. 'Carpenter is a smart, hardened old con' says Keaton, and he very quickly realized they weren't, as they suggested, just looking for some information over a coffee. He simply said that it 'sounded like murder' to him, and that he wanted an attorney – at which point, as Keaton admits, 'We knew once you've heard that word "attorney" you can't use anything else you get, so we told him we had warrants – and there was no resistance on his part: he just turns and looks at me and says, "Please don't hurt me: I've always been a model inmate." It made me want to vomit, because I though of the way he had violated these kids, the violence he had shown.'

Carpenter was whisked away, and detectives moved across to search his parents' house. His mother, who had always been such a stern disciplinarian, obviously didn't think discipline applied to her. Keaton's memory is that 'she was a complete bitch that day, an obstructionist, an obnoxious person, screaming, ranting and raving, trying to do everything she could to derail the search.'

The Santa Cruz officers had arranged a line-up, an identification parade, since of course Steve Haertle would be the absolutely crucial witness. Later in the day, Santa Cruz rang round the other forces and gave them the good news: 'An absolutely positive ID.' As Keaton says, 'You know when you go to court an attorney will tear that apart, but we knew he was off the street, and out of harm's way for other people, and all the guys got together, went out, had a couple of cocktails, a steak dinner, and celebrated. We knew the work was just beginning, we still had to go to court, and we knew that was going to be a joke, a long-drawn out process, but we in Marin County had a reprieve for a while, because they were going to Santa Cruz first.'

Santa Cruz won their case. The next trial, switched to San Diego precisely because a jury nearer San Francisco would be all too likely to have been aware of the first trial and its conclusion, had found Carpenter guilty yet again, but before he could be sentenced the jury foreperson let slip that she did indeed know about the previous conviction. The judge ruled it a mistrial, and the whole process began again. It really didn't make much difference, of course, save to the incomes of the attorneys since, as Marin DA John Posey points out, 'He's got seven death penalty sentences, and he still hasn't been executed, and he'll deny it, I think, until he dies'; but, as Rich Keaton says, 'He's off the street.'

BOBBY JOE LONG

In 14 years' service with the Sheriff's Office of Hillsborough County, Florida, Gary Terry had done almost everything from beat patrols to undercover narcotics, but until he made Lieutenant, he'd never investigated a homicide. But when his promotion came through, he was immediately put in charge of the entire unit which dealt with sex crimes, robberies – and homicides. It wasn't that big a unit – but in the early 1980s, Hillsborough County didn't have that many homicides: so few, indeed, that it was standard practice for the unit commander to go to every homicide scene, and be personally involved in the investigation.

So when two children playing in the bushes near their home on the evening of Sunday, 13 May 1984 discovered a body, the Sheriff's Office automatically called Terry at his home and asked him to respond.

'When I arrived at the scene', he says 'there was the body –

female, completely nude, lying on her stomach, hands bound behind her back, a rope ligature round her neck with kind of a leash leading off it. What really struck me was the way that she was lying – the legs had been grotesquely spread. She'd been there for almost three days, was almost completely black, in an advanced stage of decomposition; the smell was overwhelming, the skin was slipping off all over. I was standing next to colleagues with over 25 years' experience, and they looked at that body, started shaking their heads, and saying they had never seen a body displayed like that. I had that gnawing feeling in my gut – "Oh, shit; this is not good, this is a problem." '

Indeed it was – a problem which escalated so rapidly over the next few months that Terry was assigned to take a group of detectives and work exclusively on it, while others were pulled in from elsewhere in the Sheriff's office to handle any other cases. But then, as Terry rather ruefully points out, 'The public have a misconception that when a law enforcement agency has a particular problem, say a serial homicide, then all they should do is put all their resources into that crime and solve it. In the best of worlds, that would be nice, but unfortunately other criminals don't stop just because the agency has a problem. In this case, we were about to get a problem with a serial killer, but other homicides, robberies and rapes were occurring all throughout the county, so we couldn't stop everything else and just work solely on this case.'

Just prior to the discovery of this body, Hillsborough had had another murder which had been successfully resolved, but they'd done that by adopting a novel tactic. As it came in, all the forensic evidence had been flown to the FBI laboratory in Washington, involving them, as Terry puts it 'like a team member, a co-partner in the investigation, not just some sterile laboratory out-of-state.' And that's what Hillsborough did with this one – any evidence recovered was given to one of their men, who'd fly up to Washington and have it in the hands of the FBI the next day. It was to prove enormously helpful – in Terry's words, 'I think it was crucial. We did a lot of things right, and we did some things wrong, in the investigation. If anyone has an investigation of this magnitude and says they haven't made mistakes, I think they are erroneous, to say the least; but we did a lot of things right, and one of the best things was we utilized one laboratory throughout – had continuity – and the FBI lab was that lab.'

For, as they all do, Hillsborough's serial murders had begun with just one killing, and had it not been for the laboratory, investigators might never have linked some of those that followed to a single perpetrator. Eventually, the case would be solved with the enormous help of a single surviving witness – but she herself might never have been found without the aid of what Terry calls 'the silent witness – carpet fibre.'

At this early stage, however, with just one unidentified female corpse on their territory, Hillsborough went about what Gary Terry calls 'classical police investigation. We look for the person in last contact with the victim, and usually in homicide there is some correlation between victim and killer – it's only when that correlation or relationship is absent that the difficulty starts rising astronomically.'

The discovery had attracted a small mention in one of the local newspapers. That brought in calls from friends of a girl who'd gone missing from her job as an exotic dancer at one of the many bars on Nebraska Avenue in the area's big city, Tampa. Sometimes called 'the Strip', Nebraska Avenue is a place where the vast majority of the workers are women, and the vast majority of the customers are men. The first checks established that 19-year-old Ngeun Thi Long, a Laotian immigrant known on the Strip as Lana Long, had – most uncharacteristically – failed to show up for work since the previous week. Her boyfriend had not reported her missing until after the body had been found, and claimed that was because she'd walked out before after arguments – which he admitted they had had.

Sheriff's officers interviewed Lana Long's workmates, who reported to Terry that 'she was a tease; she was paid to dance for the customers, and get the customers to buy drinks for her, but when it came time to go home, she went home to her boyfriend; she was not involved in prostitution, she was not involved in narcotics, she was just doing the job that she was paid for.' (In fairness, it seems Lana's 'non-involvement' in narcotics was meant to imply she didn't deal them – but she certainly used them).

The body was indeed Lana's, and the natural first suspect was her boyfriend. While detectives concentrated on the area around the Strip and Lana's Shadow Oaks apartment, the physical evidence from the scene was sent off to Washington. It included plaster-casts of tyre-marks – which were of different tread patterns – the ligatures from Lana's body,

samples of hair and a scarf which had been with her. The FBI
found the tyre-marks interesting but couldn't come back with
immediate identifications, the ligatures yielded nothing save
the detail of the knots the killer had used, and those hairs
which were not her own were not informative. But on the
scarf, Hillsborough's newly-established regular colleague in
the Bureau, Special Agent Mike Malone, had discovered
something quite interesting: a single lustrous red trilobal
nylon fibre, probably a carpet fibre.

Lana's boyfriend, John Corcoran, was already slipping out
of the frame when a new development effectively put him
wholly in the clear. A fortnight after her body was found,
Terry got another call at home. Another body had been found,
this time in a wooded area east of Tampa. 'I still remember',
he says, 'driving towards the scene and saying to myself,
"Please don't let this victim be bound; please don't let her be
tied up."' The first thing I said to the deputy when I arrived
was, "Is this victim bound?" and he said. "Yes, sir." So now
we've gone from very rarely having victims bound in homicides to two in two weeks, so that immediately confirms our
suspicions that we have a problem on our hands.'

The second victim was also totally nude, her hands bound
to her sides, a ligature around her neck. 'But the killer didn't
stop there', recalls Terry. 'He'd also cut this victim's throat, so
severely that it nearly decapitated her: there was blood-
spatter all over her body, and he'd beaten her over the head
with a club that we found nearby. Later, the medical examiner told us there were actually three causes of death – the

severed throat, the blunt force trauma to her head, and it turned out she'd been strangled.'

In retrospect, Terry claims that he already knew 'we didn't need physical evidence to link the two, I just had a feeling right then it was the same suspect, just looking at the body and the ligatures.' But physical evidence there was: tyre-marks once more, items of clothing, ligatures, all taken north to Washington, and Malone, by hand. By now, two of the earlier tyre-marks had been identified as Goodyear Vivas, a fairly common type, but a third was proving harder to identify. Terry sent one of his men with the photographs to Goodyear's headquarters in Akron, Ohio – where an expert finally concluded that it came from a very exclusive hand-made tyre, a Vogue, which was only fitted to Cadillacs. Either someone driving one of America's most expensive cars had replaced worn tyres with a much cheaper model – or someone driving a lower-range vehicle had fitted a single, and thus probably second-hand, Vogue to just one wheel.

That raised another puzzle. It seemed that the killer had abducted two women from a busy downtown area, stripped them, bound them and then driven them miles into the countryside – which surely meant, reasoned the investigators, that he must be driving a van, not a passenger vehicle at all, or surely someone would have spotted them?

Then the FBI reported another significant finding. From the scrapings taken from the second body, they had isolated another of those lustrous red trilobal nylon fibres; and a hair, not the victim's, was that of a white person, presumed male.

The second victim in a fortnight, says Terry, 'was just like a ton of bricks had fallen on me, because now I knew it was my responsibility to manage and supervize the investigation, and we had never been involved in an investigation of this magnitude. The realization was setting in, "You've got a tiger by the tail, and you can't turn him loose because he's going to eat you alive if you do." '

Pictures of the second victim had been circulated, and she was very quickly identified (she had been discovered within hours of death, so neither Florida's weather nor its wildlife had had a chance to do much damage). Michelle Denise Simms had arrived in Tampa just one day before her murder, and immediately turned to soliciting around the Strip in order to fund her heavy cocaine habit. She'd been seen talking to two white men on Kennedy Boulevard the previous evening.

Patrol officers were told to look out for a white male with brown hair, medium to long, in possession of a knife about three inches long, a half-inch in width – determined by measuring the wound on Michelle's throat – driving a vehicle with two Goodyear Viva tyres and one Vogue. 'But', says Terry, 'we didn't mention anything about our fibre evidence, because these criminals listen to the news, they watch TV, read the newspapers, so we put safeguards in operation not to release anything about that to our own officers, to the public or the media.'

At this stage, Terry could not accept that they had someone killing women who was a stranger to them. 'We felt there had to be something we missed: there was a pimp involved, maybe, some narcotics deal gone bad or something like that. There had to be a motive, a reason to connect the deaths – but we were wrong. The one thing connecting these two cases was the fact that they had the same killer, but the killer was a stranger to them both.'

Two weeks later, while Terry's detectives were 'going in 25 different directions, running this lead, running that lead', the killer struck again – only the investigating team didn't realize it at first.

For one thing the victim, Elizabeth Loudenback, wasn't connected with the Strip's principal commercial activities. She was a 22-year-old factory worker who lived with her parents in a trailer home. For another, she had left a note before her disappearance which strongly suggested she was in a state of some apprehension – and if anything ever happened to her, it would be her boyfriend who was responsible. And she wasn't, frankly, very attractive, certainly not by Strip styles and standards.

Loudenback's strangled body was discovered in an orange grove in the east of the county, just across from Brandon County Park. Terry's account helps explain why she wasn't immediately added to the serial killer's file. 'The body was fully clothed; she was not bound. Unfortunately, she had been there for quite some time (16 days, it turned out), and the total body weight was about 31 pounds. Then we found some more differences, in the fact that her purse was missing, she was missing her ATM card, and we found that her ATM card had been used around the county by the perpetrator – you know, milking her account, taking all her money out, until finally the ATM machine ate the card; so now all of a sudden we have a homicide where robbery is a motive, and so went to her residence, and found a note which says if anything happened to her the boyfriend would be responsible. Of course, that leads us to the boyfriend, and we found out that he actually knew her PIN number for her bank card, and that they'd argued over money. He had a halfway alibi – he was supposedly at a party, but he could have left – so then we gave him a lie-detector test, and he failed it miserably. So this case was assigned to a different detective, and the evidence in this case was sent to the FBI laboratory by normal channels – in other words, by mail – and it was quite some weeks later we got notified by them that they'd found that same lustrous red trilobal nylon carpet fibre on Victim Three that they'd found on Victims One and Two.'

At this stage, the investigators were still pursuing the notion that there had to be a connection, and the red-light area would furnish it: if not a pimp or a dealer, well, maybe a regular client of prostitutes – a 'John'. That line of inquiry, seeking information from the working girls, had its problems, as Terry admits. 'Initially, they were really stand-offish, because they thought we were vice officers out to arrest them for prostitution, but once they learned we were homicide detectives trying to identify the killer of Michelle Simms, they were great sources of information. They provided names and car descriptions and licence-plate numbers of all sorts of people picking up prostitutes. Some of them were very surprising; in fact, it was good information, but we weren't able to link it to our killer.'

The team toiled on throughout July, August and well into September without making significant progress. As always, there was the desperately ambivalent attitude among them – 'Nobody wants more bodies, but if he doesn't do it again, will we ever catch him? And, even worse, maybe he has done it again – we just haven't found the bodies.' More than two million people live in the greater Tampa area, and Florida is a state to which runaways, refugees, transients and sun-seeking 'snowbirds' from all over America gravitate – the kind of people who might never be registered as missing simply because they hadn't had time to be registered as present.

On 30 September an 18-year-old whore called Chanel Devon Williams, just two days out of jail on an earlier prostitution rap, was patrolling the Strip with a friend. The understanding was that if either girl got a John, the other would hang around whichever short-stay motel was called for to check her colleague's safe return in the customary 15 or 20 minutes. Chanel's companion got the first customer, and went off with him. When she returned, Chanel was nowhere to be seen. Nor was she for another 12 days, until a group of farm-workers in the north of the county, almost at the border with neighbouring Pasco County, stopped to close a gate behind their truck. One of them, Clarence Hale, took the opportunity to walk over to an adjoining fence to relieve himself – and saw victim number four on the other side.

'When we arrived at the scene', reports Terry, 'the body was lying partially underneath the fence. There was an intense amount of insect infestation to the head – it was completely covered with insects and maggots – so we immediately knew there was some kind of external trauma inflicted on the victim, and that the body had been there for several days. She was nude, but she was not bound – but one of the great differences was that this particular victim was black. All our previous victims had been white (Long was, of course Laotian, but let's not digress) so that immediately causes discussion among us – is it the same killer, or do we have a different killer?'

Up to that point, all the FBI research on serial killings had suggested that the perpetrators stayed within their racial boundaries – white on white, black on black. Add in the fact that Chanel turned out to have been shot, not strangled, stabbed or beaten to death, and the presumption began to be made that this was not part of the series – until, that is, the FBI lab, supplied as usual with all the physical evidence available, reported back that there was a lustrous red trilobal nylon fibre on Chanel's body.

Gary Terry instantly recognized that he now had a fourth case. 'Carpet fibre has often been referred to as the silent witness', he says, 'but by its mere presence, it speaks volumes, and it spoke volumes in this case.'

Chanel had been identified easily enough – a quick finger-print check immediately turned up her arrest and imprisonment records – and the autopsy had confirmed that, gunshot or no, the killer's MO hadn't changed that much. He'd tried to strangle her, and seemed to have lost patience when she refused to die easily. But what kind of killer were they looking for?

Well, the brand-new science of profiling might just help. Quantico's experts were sent all the evidence so far collected, and reported back to Terry that he should be looking for 'a white male, aged late 20s, early 30s, presenting a macho image and assaultive behaviour, who would operate within a given geographical area until apprehended.' Not in the written report, but in a telephone call, they told Terry: 'If you don't catch him, he's going to kill again. He's maturing, he's enjoying it, he's becoming more proficient at his skill – and his skill is killing.'

In Florida's climate there is a brutal limit to what an autopsy can reveal, but there was an assumption that the killer would have raped his victims before despatching them. Certainly Hillsborough were keeping an eye on all reported sexual assaults throughout the neighbouring jurisdictions. But nobody made any connections in the early months of the investigation with a problem which had been plaguing much of Southern Florida for years: a serial offender known variously as the Ad Man Rapist and the Classified Ad Rapist. The MO was unvarying – someone advertizing household goods for sale in one of the local papers would get a call, which would establish if the vendor was female and likely to be home alone. If so, the caller would ask for directions to come by and view the items for sale, turn up, produce a knife, rape the lone woman in her home, ransack it for easily-saleable items and leave.

Although the reported total of such crimes was already

around 50, experienced detectives assumed there were probably many more, which victims had been too embarrassed to report. Although the rapist used guile, and the threat of force, he did not use excessive physical violence, let alone commit murder; and whereas the killer seemed confined to a single county, the Ad Man Rapist recognized no such boundary. The fact that it was the same man doing both was only to emerge after his arrest, because up until then the police assumption was that such a thing was impossible: as Terry says, 'From an investigative standpoint, I would have told you that there's no way you'll have a serial rapist one place, and the same one committing serial homicides in another, and not do them vice versa.'

Understandably, therefore, Hillsborough's attention was concentrated on their killer-rapist, not on the neighbours' Want-Ad rapist: all the more so when, a fortnight after Chanel's body was found, yet another one was discovered on their territory. Karen Beth Dinsfriend came from a prosperous middle-class background, but started using drugs in her early teens. She lost her job in a bank when it became clear that customers' money was paying for Karen's habit, and turned to prostitution as the easiest way to fund it, quickly acquiring an arrest record. On the night of 13 October 1984 she was picked up by a cruising John in the Strip area, forced to undress, bound and driven to the northeastern section of the county. The call to Terry came on 14 October; two men had stumbled across her body in yet another orange grove.

'She'd been wrapped in a yellow-gold acrylic bedspread, her hands were bound, her feet were bound. As soon as I saw the body, along with other detectives, we knew it was the same killer – and we actually found red trilobal nylon carpet fibre on her body.' She'd been strangled, and heavily beaten. She was quickly identified – the investigators now automatically checked fingerprints against those on file from recent prostitution arrests – but Terry and his team still had nothing but their growing collection of microscopic fibres to show for all their work.

The public unrest, and the media siege of the Sheriff's Office, grew steadily more intense. Terry managed to get a sergeant assigned full-time to handling the media inquiries, which would otherwise have taken all his time, and the FBI's Malone told him that yet again he'd found brown hairs from a white male on Karen's body. If not quite as powerfully as the carpet fibres, those at least lessened one major worry for the team: that they might, as sometimes happens, have a copycat killer, or even killers, exploiting the growing press hysteria.

Victim Six might never have been discovered at all if a 71-year-old farmer called Paul Both hadn't decided to spend Hallowe'en clearing out a ditch with a backhoe. His property was barely 50 yards from the county boundary with Pasco County, something which distinctly irritated Gary Terry when he arrived at the scene. 'You walk out of that ditch', he says, 'and you see the Welcome to Pasco County sign. We're starting to take this personal; it looks like this killer is deliberately dumping the bodies in Hillsborough County. We asked ourselves, "Why can't this guy go a few yards down the damn road and put the body in another county?"'

Kimberly Hoops had been in that ditch for some time. Although Terry says 'in this case, we didn't find any physical or trace evidence' – and, indeed, the mummified remains were not identified until after the eventual arrest – he also says, 'But we didn't have to – we just had the feeling, you've seen five cases up to now, you see this sixth case, you know it's him again.'

Although it couldn't be claimed the investigators were making significant progress – until they identified a suspect, whose carpet and hair matched Malone's samples, they scarcely could – morale was high. For all the team, reports Terry, 'this was our sole purpose in life; to solve this case, stop this individual killing – that's all we were living and breathing, day in, day out. That was the unique thing about this case – you could have asked officers to work 24 hours a day, seven days a week, and they would. And some of them did. The sacrifice was unbelievable, but those men and women were prepared to do it, because of what was at stake – people's lives.'

The sacrifices are undeniable. Terry decided that one possible means of flushing out their killer was to conduct a decoy operation. 'We selected two women deputies, dressed them in very alluring clothing, equipped them with body transmitters and got them to pose as prostitutes in some of our high prostitution areas. There were teams of undercover officers assigned to protect and watch them, while they identified cars and drivers coming to solicit them. They were instructed NOT to get into a car – just engage the person in conversation, tell our undercover monitoring officers what the colour of the car is, the description of the car, the licence number, the description of the suspect. I was so concerned at the risk, I went out to sit with the surveillance team, and watched this young lady. We did such a good job, one night we had traffic backed up down one street and around the corner, of people lined up to talk to this particular female officer. Several years later, she came to me and confided that was the most frightened she had ever been in her life – when you think about it, it's like putting a worm on a hook and putting it out there and hoping for a bite.'

Just in case they did get a bite, Terry had issued specific orders. The female officers were not to get into any car unless they were threatened by a gun or knife, but if they did, he 'instructed the surveillance officers to stop that car at all costs, to ram it or whatever they had to do – and I went on to explain to them that if they were not successful in stopping that car, then they might as well leave their badge and commission on the dashboard, because that was where mine was going to be if we lost an undercover officer.'

In retrospect, Hillsborough County has to be applauded for its willingness, as a small, semi-rural agency, to try any and every new method to cope with a case which might at the time have baffled any of the world's biggest police forces. Building a dedicated relationship with the FBI labs was absolutely central to the eventual cracking of the case; the decoy operation was at least as well-organized as any the NYPD could mount; and they also took on board a military technique which owed something to the jungle warfare of Vietnam. 'We flew sorties with a helicopter', explains Terry, 'which we equipped with an infra-red device that would detect objects giving off heat. We actually had to borrow that from an intelligence agency. It flew sorties late at night, into the early morning hours, over the remote sites of the county. When you switch off a car engine, it gives off an immense amount of heat, so the thought was, as you fly over, you find a car parked in a wooded area; it's maybe the killer, dumping another body. It's a good technique, and it worked – we found some very surprised people in some very unusual areas at two, three o'clock in the morning. They couldn't understand why a deputy sheriff was suddenly in the middle of the pasture. A good technique, but not successful from our point of view.'

Whatever the constant observation of the red-light district, and the aerial patrol of the woodland back-roads, was doing to inhibit Florida's adultery rate, it still wasn't tracking the killer. Nothing daunted, Hillsborough – which in 1984 certainly wasn't a computerized agency – sent a detective out to buy a personal computer for the task force.

Finally, however, the killer relented on Hillsborough – it was Pasco County Sheriff's Office which got the call, on 6 November, to yet another rural setting where two women had made a horrific discovery while taking a gentle jaunt on horseback. The field they'd entered was strewn with body parts, and pungent with the stink of decomposition. Virginia Lee Johnson, another worker on the Strip, had been there for around two weeks, and the animals and elements had wrought havoc on her remains. But Pasco County knew quite enough about Hillsborough's problem to fire off an immediate call to Terry's task force. It looked like him again.

Perhaps we should recall the quite appalling experiences which homicide detectives in hot and humid climates are forced to undergo. Gary Terry evokes it with nauseating clarity: 'There is no way to describe the horrific smell of a decaying body. You are looking at another human being, and you see the insects, and you can smell the smell. I can close my eyes right now and smell that smell. Any homicide investigator can tell you the same thing – it never goes away; it never goes away. I can remember times coming in and actually taking the clothes off that I wore at the scene, and leaving them outside, having them washed the next day. The smell gets in them, and I can pick up the same suit and smell the victim now. That never leaves you.'

What's more, investigators on a peculiarly repellent crime can find that they, too, carry a metaphorical stink. Terry recalls that at the height of the inquiry, 'Myself and other detectives were going to the break room: we'd sit down, have a cup of coffee, and other people would get up and sit somewhere else, because they didn't want to be associated with us. It was like there was a cloud on top of us, and it was raining bodies every two weeks.'

Pasco County's body was reported on the local radio even before they had got through to Terry on the phone. 'As soon as I heard it', he says 'I asked two of my detectives to take a

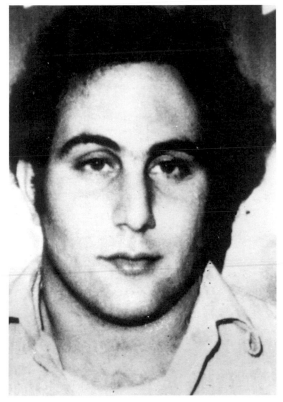

ABOVE: David
Berkowitz, aka
Son of Sam, is
arrested.
(Topham Picturepoint)

LEFT: Berkowitz
terrorized New
York for an
entire summer.
(Topham Picturepoint)

Angelo BUONO & Kenneth BIANCHI

TOP: The Hillside Stranglers — left, Angelo Buono,
right, Kenneth Bianchi.

Cindy Hudspeth's Datsun, off the road at
Angeles Crest, February 1978. Cindy's body is
still in the trunk.

David CARPENTER

Marin County's
Sergeant Rich Keaton,
the man who finally
arrested David
Carpenter.

David Carpenter, the Trailside Killer,
still sits on Death Row. (AP Photo)

Bobby Joe LONG

BOBBY JOE LONG   SERIAL
                   KILLER
                   Aged 39 at time of arrest

SHERIFF'S OFFICE
TAMPA, FLA.

Bobby Joe Long immediately after his arrest.

Gary Terry, of Hillsbrough County Sheriff's Office,
who led the hunt for Bobby Joe.

Beverly Hills
detective Les
Zoeller, who had
a hunch about the
Menendez Brothers
from almost the
first moment.

Lyle and Erik Menendez on trial — on Erik's right,
defence attorney Leslie Abramson. (Rex/SIPA/Juan Venegez)

Ivan MILAT

LEFT: Commander Clive Small of New South Wales Police,
who led the investigation into the Backpacker Murders.

RIGHT: His quarry - Ivan Milat.

ABOVE: Milat's Nissan
Patrol, which Paul Onions
could never forget.

ABOVE: Milat's garage,
stuffed with property
linking him to the
murders, including Simone
Schmidl's yellow t-shirt.

Detectives Gil
Carillo and Frank
Salerno, partners
in the pursuit of
the Nightstalker.

The Nightstalker
himself, Richard
Ramirez, makes
the satanic sign
as he leaves
Court and heads
for San Quentin
Prison.
(AP Photo/Alan Greth)

Aileen WUORNOS

LEFT: Aileen Wuornos,
manacled and in prison
denims, on trial.
(AP Photo/Peter Cosgrove)

ABOVE: Aileen Wuornos's
deadly nine-shot .22
pistol, recovered from the
waters of Rose Bay.

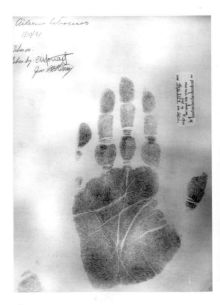

ABOVE AND LEFT: Wuornos's fingerprints were
instrumental in bringing her to trial.

drive up there, stay outside the crime-scene and call me back. Well, they did – the first thing they said was, "It's him again." I said, "What do you mean?" and they said, "Well, they've got a body scattered over almost an acre, but they still have ligatures attached – it's him again; the same killer."'

Terry's immediate response was to ask Pasco County, who normally used a lab of their own, to despatch all evidence from the scene to Malone at the FBI. They did – and Malone called back to both agencies to report that he'd found that same red trilobal nylon carpet fibre, despite the ravages of two weeks' exposure. Different jurisdiction, maybe; but same killer, without question.

On Friday, 9 November, a meeting was held for investigating officers from all the agencies now involved – Hillsborough, Pasco, the City of Tampa Police Department and the state-wide Florida Department of Law Enforcement. It was agreed that a joint task force should be set up, and begin work on the following Monday.

The killer might just as well have been at the meeting.

That Monday, sign-painter Drake Reed was asked to repair a road sign off Orient Road in the city of Tampa. When he climbed his ladder, his eye was caught by something in the small spinney nearby. When he went to investigate, he discovered the dreadfully battered body of a young woman, spread-eagled on her back, with faecal matter on her legs.

Tampa called Terry almost the moment Drake Reed rang in. When he got to the overpass, he didn't need to get too close to the corpse to know that this was Number Eight. 'You could see the ligature marks from 20 feet away. As soon as I saw it, I knew it was him again. And the detectives were actually finding red trilobal nylon carpet fibre on the body.' What they also found – her killer, for once, having left most of her clothing at the dump-site – was her driver's licence in her jeans – she'd been 21 years old, her name was Kim Marie Swann, and early enquiries established that she had worked at one time at the Sly Fox Lounge. Officers who visited her mother to break the news reported having learned that Kim had told her mother she'd actually known two of the earlier victims. Him again – no question – even before the FBI rang back to confirm the carpet fibres.

Of course, as Terry says, 'By now we were going crazy with carpet fibres. We'd gone to every motel and hotel on Nebraska, Kennedy, 50th Street and Interstate Four – every location we can think of – looking for fibre evidence. We're stopping cars, we're inundating the laboratory with carpet fibre samples, and every time they keep coming back, "No; no match." '

The City of Tampa did have, meanwhile, another intriguing crime on its hands. On the night of 3 November, sometime between the abductions of Pasco County's still unidentified body and that of Kim Swann, another young woman had been kidnapped as she cycled home from her night-time job at a doughnut shop in the general area of the Strip. Seventeen-year-old Lisa McVey wasn't a prostitute, or even an exotic dancer, but she had been forced at gunpoint into a car, in which she was promptly stripped and blindfolded.

But she hadn't been killed: repeatedly raped and sodomized, kept in captivity for around 26 hours, but not killed. What's more, she'd managed, despite the blindfold, to amass a host of small clues as to where she'd been taken – and in what vehicle. It didn't fit the MO of the serial killer, or indeed the Ad Man Rapist, but in the new climate of co-operation Tampa agreed to send all physical evidence to the FBI – and to share all that Lisa had recollected.

One: the car she'd been forced into was a dark red colour. Two: it had red carpet, but white upholstery. Three: the location she'd been taken to was an apartment block, also with red carpet. Four: she'd peeked under the blindfold while in the car and seen the word 'Magnum' on the dashboard. Five: when her kidnapper had taken her away from the apartment, and driven her off to an anonymous parking lot to leave her, alive, he'd stopped first to get cash from an ATM, then to get fuel, where she'd managed to see motel signs for both a Howard Johnson's and for a Quality Inn.

Gary Terry and a colleague, desperate for any help they could get, had flown up to Atlanta, Georgia, where the city police had managed to solve a series of child murders with the help of fibre evidence. They even tracked round the various carpet factories in the area in the hope they might get an identifying lead. But the lead came by phone. Terry was actually in the office of the Director General of Atlanta's Bureau of Investigation when the urgent call was patched through to him.

It was Hillsborough. They had an urgent call from Malone at the FBI, who desperately needed to reach Terry. 'I called Washington, and asked Mike what he needed. His first words were, "Gary, are you sitting down?" I said "Why?", and he said, "Because we just had a fibre match on your homicide cases. We just matched a fibre sample from a Tampa rape case to your homicide cases." And as Mike then said, "If you find that fibre in the McVey case, you've found the source of fibre in your homicides." '

Terry immediately raced to the airport to fly home – leaving his colleague, Corporal Lee Baker, to make the long drive back in their patrol car – because he now knew that they were closing in. The laboratory's evidence was suddenly transformed from arid science to vital clue – if the living witness, Lisa, could point them in the right direction. Which – astonishingly, given her ordeal – she could.

Top of the list was the car. Lisa may not have been a car buff, but her recollection of that 'Magnum' scrolled on to the dashboard told the police instantly that the suspect's vehicle could only be a Dodge Magnum. While police patrol cars were told to look out for any model of that type in red or maroon, the State's licensing bureau was asked to print out all known registrations.

The two approaches struck gold almost simultaneously. The license bureau informed Hillsborough that there were precisely 478 Dodge Magnums registered in Florida. Two detectives cruising Nebraska Avenue had already seen one, pulled it over, very politely explained to the driver that a similar car had been involved in a hit-and-run accident, asked for his licence, noted his name and address and, with permission, taken a Polaroid photograph of him.

The driver's name was Billy Joe Long. The registration list included a Billy Joe Long. The Polaroid photograph, shown to Lisa McVey, produced a positive identification. Robert J. Long, as he preferred to be called when trying to distance himself from his West Virginia hillbilly origins, was finally in the frame.

There was only one automated telling machine in a location near both a Howard Johnson's and a Quality Inn – close to the campus of the University of Florida. The investigators rapidly subpoenaed the bank to discover who'd used it in the early morning hours of 4 November, and a detective flew down to their headquarters in Jacksonville to pick up the information. There hadn't been that many transactions – but the one that stood out a mile was by a customer called Bobby Joe Long.

As Terry says, 'By now, the investigation was going 90 miles an hour. We've got 45 or 50 officers assigned to the task force, so of course we go to the State Attorney and say, "OK, here's the information – kidnapping, sexual assault, false imprisonment – but he says, 'Oh, no; you've got kidnapping, sexual assault, false imprisonment, but you don't have enough for homicide." He authorizes us to get a warrant on the lesser charges, and we send out a surveillance team to watch Mr Long at his apartment.'

As the undercover police kept watch, they saw Long make several trips out of the back of the apartment building into a wooded area, where he was observed throwing various items into a rubbish skip. While Terry was busy getting a search warrant for Long's car and apartment the suspect again left, got into his car and drove to a nearby service station, where he proceeded to vacuum the car's interior. It had become fairly obvious that he knew the net was closing, and was trying to dispose of as much evidence as he could, while he could. However, the moment he left the service station, a detective raced in and snatched the vacuum. Long's next stop was at a cinema, showing *Missing In Action*. He proceeded to watch the movie, unaware that there was a detective in front of him, one either side of him, and another behind. Outside, other detectives from the task force had been joined by FBI agents, and had taken the opportunity to crawl under Long's Dodge Magnum in the car-park – from where they radioed back to Terry that it had two Goodyear Viva tyres and one Goodyear Vogue.

'As soon as he said that', recalls Terry, 'we all knew, "That's our guy" – the same tyres we'd identified back in May at the scene of Michelle Simms' murder. So now all is crescendoing, and we get the signal to make the arrest.'

The movie over, Long left the cinema – to be met by a dozen or more officers with guns drawn, shouting at him to get down on the ground. As Gary Terry says, 'He didn't provide any resistance, immediately complied and went down, and it's a good thing that he did, because we had many officers out there...' the implication being pretty clear that if Long had shown any sign of resistance whatsoever, the taxpayers of Florida would have been saved a lot of time and trouble trying him.

The car was immediately impounded and taken off for exhaustive examination while Bobby Joe, having been read his rights, was driven back to his apartment, where he had the right to be present during the search. In front of the block there were not only more than 50 officers ('Everybody', says Terry, 'wanted to see what this guy looked like'), but all the neighbours. The sight was too much for Long, who simply refused to get out of the police car and opted instead to be taken directly to the Sheriff's Office.

At this stage, of course, he was only under arrest on the Lisa McVey charges, so the task of interviewing him presented a delicate challenge. As it happened, he immediately confessed to the kidnapping of Lisa McVey, and even expressed his concern for her; but what the interviewers were after – they were two of Terry's most experienced detectives – was to see if he'd give anything away when they raised the subject of the murders.

'Initially', remembers Terry, 'he denied it. But then the officers began explaining to him about trace evidence, forensic science, and while that was happening the FBI agents were processing what we'd got from the apartment and the car. Then they called, said they had a positive match on the red lustrous trilobal nylon fibre – a conclusive match from the carpet in Long's car to the fibres found at the various homicides. So the officers went back in to Long and told him all about the hair evidence, the tyre evidence, the carpet evidence, the blood evidence – and he confesses to the homicides, and begins detailing all the homicide scenes.'

In fact, of course, Long told the officers about at least one murder they didn't know had been committed – a missing waitress called Vicky Elliott – before he suddenly clammed up, and said he thought he'd better get an attorney. Which is one reason he's still conducting interminable legal battles from Death Row.

Another is that Pasco County had been able to make a case against him for half a dozen of the Ad Man Rapes, which went to trial first – and for which Bobby Joe got a total of 693 years.

Since his arrest, the suspicion has grown that he probably killed at least three other women, and that his Want-Ad rapes could number anything from 50 to 100.

So what does Gary Terry make of him? 'Killing, to him, was just a means to an end; what he really enjoyed, in my belief, was the terror and torture and domination he could see in their eyes. That's what really gave him a high. A predator – an absolute predator.'

RICHARD RAMIREZ –
THE NIGHTSTALKER

The summer of 1985 was the hottest Southern California had known for 100 years. The inhabitants of Los Angeles County, with its 96 cities, would have liked nothing better than to have slept with their windows open, only the mesh screens in place to let in the air and keep out the bugs. But for three horrendous months they turned instead to padlocks and bars, desperate to protect themselves from a burglar whose thefts seemed almost an afterthought to his murders, mutilations and rapes.

Few things are as terrifying as the thought that a stranger might, at any moment, break into your home and subject your family to unimaginable violence – but that was how every Angeleno had to live while the killer whom the media called 'The Nightstalker' was on the rampage.

As the crimes mounted up, the fragments of evidence – and of paranoid rumour – merely fed the horror. It seemed the killer dressed all in black, was a dedicated Satanist, suffered both from bad breath and body odour, offered an indiscriminate threat of sexual violence to children, young adults and the elderly, and fitted the secret prejudice of many English-speaking Californians – a Mexican. He was prepared to shoot, to stab, to bludgeon, to beat and kick to death. What's more, in the state where everybody drives, he struck everywhere from well south of Los Angeles to San Francisco, though mainly in the communities which ring the city of LA itself.

Always scrupulous to wear cotton gloves, he left few fingerprints. Adept at prowling in the dark, he offered few useful sightings. As good a car-thief as he was a burglar, he seldom needed to use the same vehicle for very long. Willing to use any weapon and take any victim, he confused many investigators who simply couldn't imagine that one criminal would so vary their MO, and resisted colleagues' insistence that there was, indeed, just one 'Nightstalker'.

Frankly, if he'd thought to change his shoes more often, and looked more carefully at where he trod, he might still be on the loose, instead of sitting out his 13th year on Death Row: which, so far, amounts to just one year for each of his 13 murder convictions – and, as with any major serial killer, the lingering suspicion that there might be other deaths for which he'll never be held to account.

Certainly, nobody imagined that a serial killer was at large back in June 1984, when 79-year old Jennie Vincow was killed. She lived in a small apartment block in the modest

Los Angeles suburb of Glassell Park, while her son Jack had an apartment on the upper floor. On the night of 27 June, Jennie's apartment was burglarized, but nothing much was taken – because Jennie didn't have very much to take. Instead, the intruder stabbed her repeatedly, and slashed her throat so deeply she was almost decapitated. The following day, her son came down to bring her lunch, and discovered the carnage. The Los Angeles Police Department responded, and found some fingerprints on the window which had been used to gain access: not helpful, in those days of manual comparison, unless and until there was an actual suspect. Other than that, there was nothing of much use at all. The investigation quietly subsided into the file.

However, the autopsy told pathologist Dr Joseph Cogan one chilling thing. Whoever had done the stabbing knew their business: had, he felt sure, done something like it before.

Which must for ever leave a lingering doubt that the Nightstalker really didn't strike again until March 1985. Murder is not uncommon in the sleazier parts of LA and, as the Hillside stranglings had shown, plenty of investigators can adopt a fairly laid-back attitude when the victim seems of low status, a whore, drug-dealer or gang member; what the cynical cops mark in their notebooks as 'NHI' – No Humans Involved.

Still, all the courts ever passed judgment on over that long period was an attempted murder and two murders on the night of 17 March 1985 – St Patrick's Day, as Detective Gil Carillo of the Los Angeles County Sheriff's Department rather incongruously remembers it. He's of Mexican descent, and the victims were variously of Japanese, Taiwanese and Hispanic descent, and so unlikely to have been making much of Ireland's biggest celebration.

Carillo got the call at about 10.40 in the evening. 'They told me to respond to a call; gave me the address. It was a homicide – just another murder in the county. The crime scene was a condominium complex in the suburb of Rosemead. The garage door opened to the south, the front door opened to the north. At the threshold of the garage was a baseball cap with 'AC/DC' written on the front of it, and as you entered the condo from the door that led to the garage there was blood-spattering and a bottle of water. The blood trail led out of the garage and all the way round to the front of the condo, and into the kitchen area where the victim was, Dayle Okazaki. She had sustained what appeared to be a single gunshot wound. She was lying in a pool of blood.

'Further examination showed a considerable amount of blood droplets, and evidence that whoever had made the call to the Sheriff's Office had used the telephone inside the residence to do so, because there was blood over the phone. At that stage I thought it was a routine, mundane murder, and you're not thinking about suspects; you're looking at a crime scene as a homicide investigator, and it takes total concentration, because that crime scene tells you a story, so you're not looking at who, you're looking at what.'

In fact, if Carillo was making any guesses at that stage they were along the lines of a *crime passionel* – Dayle had obviously been a very attractive young woman and the killing looked deliberate, not committed in the course of another crime. But the caller who had left her blood on the phone turned out to be Dayle's flatmate, another attractive young woman called Maria Hernandez. She had just driven home, and was about to shut the garage door when she became aware of a man entering from the driveway. He was pointing a gun at her, and she instinctively put up her hands to shield her head: in her hands were her car and house-keys, and the bullet struck them, merely injuring her hand. She fell to the ground and played dead. He had then gone into the house and shot Dayle, turned on his heel and left, where he'd spotted Maria who was coming round the walkway in search of help. Although he pointed the gun at her again, he decided instead to make his escape, jumped into the car he had stolen earlier that evening and sped away – leaving both a witness and a cap which suggested he was a rock fan.

The following morning, Carillo got a surprise. As soon as Maria Hernandez's mother arrived, she greeted him by name – not only had she been a neighbour of his family's when he was a child, but Carillo's parents had actually been Maria's sponsors at her baptism. Gil and Maria hadn't seen each other since their infancy, but at the trial, to cast doubt upon her evidence, as Carillo says, 'the defence teams tried to raise an issue that I may have given her information or helped her out in some way because I had known her.'

But he was also puzzling why the killer should have let her survive, after shooting Dayle. 'It was different – don't ask me why I thought it was different – and I told my partner, "This is not your routine, mundane murder."' It certainly wasn't. Carillo and his partner heard that day that there had been another murder the previous night, less than an hour after the one they were handling, in nearby Monterey Park: another single woman of Asian origin, Veronica Yu; also, it turned out, shot with a .22 pistol.

As a matter of routine practice, the sheriff's officers called the Monterey police. 'We touched bases', is the way Carillo puts it. 'The way business goes, we need to concentrate on our murder, not work somebody else's, and they were of the opinion it was a boyfriend – their murder was a boyfriend/girlfriend squabble – and whoever was on the phone just hung up.' The thought still hung in the air that two Asians had been killed and a Hispanic allowed to live, but in one case a man had entered a house, while Veronica Yu had apparently been dragged out of her car and shot on the sidewalk. Still, the two murders had happened within an hour of each other, probably not more than three miles apart... Nevertheless, if Monterey thought they had a line, Carillo left them to it.

He went instead to interview Maria at the Beverly Hospital. She had absolutely no idea who might have wanted to kill her flatmate, or indeed, herself, but she was very willing to help a police artist put a composite together. Carillo had it with him when he paid a visit the next day to the East Los Angeles station of the Sheriff's department and he showed it around, just in case it rang any bells. It did.

Detective Rene Galindo also had a composite of a suspect – and they looked alike. But Galindo's case wasn't a murder of an adult – it was the kidnapping and sexual assault of a 12-year-old girl in Montebello, which is about five or six miles away from Rosemead. Nevertheless, the physical descriptions given by the young girl and by Maria Hernandez tallied as closely as the artist's impressions.

The following week the killer moved to Whittier, yet another of those affluent little cities which ring the sprawl of Los Angeles proper. Hitherto, its only claim to notoriety had been as the home town of Richard Milhous Nixon, but on the night of 26 March 1985, two of its more respectable citizens were murdered in horrifying fashion. Vincent and Maxine Zazzara were both asleep when the intruder squeezed his way in through a small window in their utility room. Vincent, 66, had dozed off in the den, while his 44-year old wife had gone to bed. Contact wounds were to show that Vincent had been shot in the head while he still lay on the sofa.

Maxine was woken by the noise, and the irruption into her bedroom of the burglar, pointing his pistol. He tied her up, and then began to ransack the room for valuables – at which point, Maxine seems to have dragged out a shotgun from under the bed and tried to shoot him. Unfortunately, the gun was empty – unloaded, perhaps, by Vincent because their small grandchildren had been visiting the previous weekend – and her action appears to have enraged the intruder, who not only shot Maxine three times with his .22 pistol, but then took a knife from the kitchen and began to mutilate her. He stabbed her in the throat, the stomach, and the pubic area, cut a crude T-shape in her chest as though he had tried to hack out her heart – and then not merely cut out her eyeballs, but took them away with him.

The Zazzaras owned a pizzeria in the town, and it was the manager's custom to drop off the takings at their house on his way home. On the evening of the 27th, although the lights were on, he could get no answer to the doorbell, so pushed the bag of money through the mail-slot. He later telephoned, but got no reply. Worried, he returned to the house on the morning of the 28th, and again could get no answer. Unwilling to enter the house alone, although the door was not fully shut, he drove off to another of the Zazzaras' shops and asked the manager there to return with him.

As soon as they saw the appalling, blood-splashed scene, they ran out to call the emergency services. For some inexplicable reason, the first vehicle to arrive was a fire-truck, but it was soon followed by the Sheriff's department, who sealed off the house and garden to await the homicide detectives and the Coroner's men.

At one and the same time, the case was about to become more confusing and yet to yield its first significant clue – and move sharply up the scale of priorities.

First, the clue. Immediately beneath the window which had been forced was a flowerbed: in the earth, a number of footprints. Very quickly it was established that some were Vincent Zazzara's – but the others certainly were not. They were, for a start, very big – size eleven-and-a-half – but also very distinctively ridged. Photographs and plaster-casts were taken for expert appraisal.

Carillo hadn't been alerted to the Whittier killings at first, but within a couple of days he was, since the weapon had been a .22, just as it had been with Hernandez, Okazaki and Yu. What's more, the Sheriff's Office decided one of their most experienced senior officers should look into the growing list of crimes to see if there were any similarities. The choice fell on Sergeant Frank Salerno, the man who had, with the LAPD's Bob Grogan, caught the Hillside Stranglers. Salerno had approached Carillo a few months earlier and asked if he'd like to become his partner when his current partner retired: as Carillo says, 'This was a scene out of a movie, you know; when you see the girl that's just been asked by the hunk at the dance if he can date her again in the future? Frank Salerno was the guru, the leader, I had heard nothing but good things about him. I was like a kid in a candy store – I mean, it doesn't get any better.'

The Nightstalker therefore brought forward what was due to happen anyway, since Carillo was already handling part of the caseload which Salerno was to examine and oversee. However, what confronted the two detectives had still to be clarified and agreed.

A series of killings by a domestic intruder who uses the same weapon makes a plausible scenario to experienced cops: they're perfectly prepared to accept that they may have a single serial offender on their hands. But this one was beginning to go off at variety of tangents. Carillo already had the puzzle of the two composites, one from Hernandez and another from a child. Now they heard from Montebello that their inquiries into the abduction of the 12-year-old had turned up the fact that the LAPD were investigating an abduction of a ten-year-old girl in the city, and that a five-year-old had managed to escape a similar approach. As Carillo says, 'At no time in criminal history has one man been so diverse as to go across the line between paedophilia and adult homicides.'

Meanwhile,the shoe-print at the Zazzaras' had been identified. It was an Avia Model 440. When the Montebello investigators revealed that they too had a footprint, taken from wet concrete which the suspect had crossed after assaulting the little girl, and it was indeed a size eleven-and-a-half Avia, criminal history began to seem open to a dramatic revision.

By now, four agencies were involved – the Sheriff's department, Monterey Park, the City of Montebello and the LAPD: not uncommon in America, let alone California, which boasts 63 separate police jurisdictions, but not helpful. Indeed, Monterey Park had already recovered the stolen vehicle which the killer had used on the night of the Okazaki killing, failed to realize what they had and returned it to its owner without even dusting it for fingerprints.

When Carillo heard that detectives from Montebello, Monterey Park and yet another jurisdiction, Pico Rivera, were having a meeting to compare notes on the child abductions each had under investigation, he went along with some colleagues. Believers in the rigid patterns of any criminal's behaviour had now to take on board a further complication: Monterey Park had a case of a 12-year-old boy being kidnapped and sexually assaulted. However, the descriptions remained very similar. At the meeting was an FBI agent, David Granish. Carillo put forward his theory linking the murders with the abductions, and Granish said he'd send all the different agencies' reports back to the profiling section of the FBI in Quantico, Virginia. He didn't say, and Carillo only found out later on, that Granish didn't believe Carillo's theory held water, and so never bothered to let Quantico have his material. In fact, just about the only officer involved who was prepared to accept that Carillo might be right was Frank Salerno.

Meanwhile, another distraction had cropped up. The Sheriff's Office had received a report, as Gil remembers, that 'some guy is following girls around in East Los Angeles, and he matched the general statistics of the bad guy, wearing dark clothing, had a musky odour, stained, gapped teeth, so a surveillance team was put on the man and he was bizarre. He was hiding and following women: at one time he picked up a prostitute and then threw her out of the car half a block later – it turned out it was a transvestite. He'd go and park on streets, wait for pedestrians, and if nobody came along in half an hour he'd start up and move to another location. We thought we were on to something, but it turned out there's a lot of strange people all over the world, and we certainly have our fair share of freaks in Los Angeles County, and this was just one of them. We got a search warrant on his house, and a court order to get him for a line-up, and he wasn't picked at the line-up... He did have some bizarre things at home, but he just wasn't my suspect. He was eventually arrested later on for other things, but not my guy.'

If the Nightstalker carried out any crimes in April – which, as a drug-using, unemployed burglar, seems likely – none came to the attention of the informal squad which Salerno was now running. The next call to Carillo came on 14 May – from Monterey Park again. An intruder had broken into the home of an elderly Japanese-American couple, William and Lillian Doi, killed William with shots to the head from a .22 and then raped and beaten 56-year old Lillian, having used thumb-cuffs on her – something a little out of the ordinary, save only that some of the children assaulted earlier reported exactly the same thing.

'When I got to the scene', reports Carillo, 'I was met outside the residence by a member of the Monterey Park Police Department, and it was very obvious to me I was not welcome at his crime scene. The attitude was, "Here's Big Brother" because it was a smaller agency, and Sheriff's Homicide was there. He said, "What are you doing here?", and I just told him "Good morning" and that I was called there by my department, and a request had come from Monterey Park for me to take a look at the scene to see if it had anything to do with what we were working. He immediately told me that he didn't call me – that he was the handling investigator – so I said, "Fine; can I just have your name in case somebody asks me, I can tell them that I came and I wasn't needed", so he reluctantly said why didn't I just come in and take a look. I remember asking him if every piece of evidence had been photographed in its place, and he said, "Yes", so I said, "Well, you might want to think about picking up some of your evidence, because there's somebody I can see standing on a cartridge case."'

As a parting shot that may have given Carillo both professional and personal satisfaction after his graceless welcome, but there was worse to come from the endless petty particularisms of the smaller forces. As Gil reveals, it was only when looking through Monterey's photographs of the Doi scene much later on – 'after we had filed the case, in September' – that he discovered a footprint had been found in the garden. An Avia.

A fortnight later the killer struck in Monrovia, in the San Gabriel Valley. Fortunately, perhaps, the Monrovia force knows its limitations, and contracts out its more serious crimes to the Sheriff's Office, rather than defending its territory. The victims were two very elderly sisters, Mabel Bell, 83, and Nettie Lang, 81. Nettie was an invalid, but Mabel (universally known as 'Ma Bell') was an active and spirited woman who found time to play bridge three times a week in between being an enthusiastic grandmother to 12 grandchildren. Like Maxine Zazzara, she very probably resisted the Nightstalker – who not only beat in her skull with a hammer, but then used her bedside clock's flex to electrocute her. He then raped and sodomized Nettie before declaring his loyalty to Satan by daubing a pentagram not only on Mabel's bedroom wall, but on the back of her thigh. He drank a soft drink, ate a banana and left with a pillowcase full of their humble belongings.

The following day their long-time gardener Carlos Valenzuela called, but got no answer. The next day he tried again, noticed uncollected newspapers on the porch and went in to see if the old ladies were sick. Astonishingly, both were still – just – alive. Indeed, Nettie was to survive, although her sister did not. Monrovia Police were notified, and called in the Sheriff's Office – but since there were distinct differences in the MO from the previous Nightstalker cases, the detectives who attended were not from Salerno and Carillo's specialized team. One of them noted that there was a bloody footprint on the smashed bedside clock, but did not identify it as an Avia – which it was eventually found to be.

During the two-and-a-half days the Monrovia victims lay undiscovered in their home, the killer had switched his attentions to Burbank, yet another distinct jurisdiction, and a community best known for its film and TV studios. This time, having used a cat-flap to unbolt the door, he raped and sodomized 44-year-old Carol Kyle, having first handcuffed her and her 11-year-old son Mark. But he not only let them live – he left the handcuff keys on a shelf. Once more, the pattern didn't fit the record, and when a composite drawn up by an artist from the LAPD didn't look like any others circulating around the various agencies, nobody in Burbank made any connections, nor any calls to Salerno.

Next time, there was no possibility of Salerno and Carillo being kept in the dark. On the night of 15 June the

Nightstalker switched his attentions to Pico Rivera. The house he chose was that of John and Susan Rodriguez, and it wasn't just that Carillo's mother's house was barely three blocks away which guaranteed attention – Rodriguez was himself a Sheriff's deputy. Although John had gone to bed, Susan was still nodding in front of the TV set when she heard a noise as of a window being pushed up: she called to her husband, who not only denied that he'd opened a window but pointed out that the window she'd indicated had not opened since he'd painted it, a little over-enthusiastically, two years earlier. The noise of their conversation startled the Nightstalker, who had indeed been chipping away at the paint with a screwdriver, and he fled.

Both Salerno and Carillo, among their other duties, gave lectures to young deputies on essential techniques such as interviewing, interrogations – and crime scene investigations. Early that morning, they got a call from a patrol deputy at the Rodriguez home. 'He'd not only taken a class of mine at the Academy', says Carillo, 'but had also seen a footprint – an Avia footprint. So I responded out there, and it really was quite comical, because this young deputy had houses on both sides taped off, so nobody was going to get in there whatsoever, and he'd covered this footprint with a big box to make sure nobody, nor weather, wind nor animals, was going to destroy it.'

Their suspect was, of course, long gone. Frustrated by the Rodriguez failure, he turned again to child abduction, in the LAPD area – but the little girl screamed so loud that he ran off – as a neighbour, alerted by the noise, looked out of her window and promptly rang 911. The Nightstalker then ignored one of the basic rules of crime – which can be summed up as 'Never boost on the way out'. In other words, if you've committed one crime, do not draw attention to yourself by committing another, however slight, as you make your escape. He went through a red light.

LAPD motorcycle traffic officer John Stavros saw him, turned on his siren and set off in pursuit. Stavros didn't spot the errant driver throwing a gun out of the window before he actually pulled over, and when he'd dismounted and ordered the offender out of his car he readily accepted that the man had left his driving documents at home, and merely told him to remain with his hands on the hood of the car while he went back to his bike to radio in the false name and address which he'd been given plus, of course, the licence plate of the Toyota car. The Nightstalker not only knew that it was a stolen car, and that the name and address wouldn't stand up to checking: he actually heard from Officer Stavros's radio an all-points bulletin about the attempted abduction, and the stolen Toyota thought to be involved. But with the single-minded concentration which traffic cops all over the world can sometimes display, Stavros was still getting out his pad of tickets when the driver, having first drawn a pentagram in the dust on the hood, took off as fast as his legs could carry him.

Stavros failed to catch him, and arranged for the car to be towed to the LAPD pound. He didn't ask for it to be searched and finger-printed and when, later, Salerno and Carillo heard about it, they were refused access to it, and not told that on the floor were a dental appointment card, and a small notebook with half a dozen phone numbers. By the time they did discover that, three weeks later, the baking California sun had destroyed all traces of any fingerprints on the vehicle and three more murders, an attempted murder and a rape had been added to the list.

When they did learn about it, the dental surgery was watched for the 'Richard Mena' who, they discovered from Dr Peter Leung, would be in need of urgent treatment for his painful abscesses. But too late – he had actually attended the surgery after Officer Stavros had impounded the car, but four days before Los Angeles finally allowed Salerno's squad to gain access.

Still, there were the signature footprints. A young criminalist – a forensic science technician – called Gerald Burke was told to get on to that Avia shoe. He remembers that it was a pure fluke the maker had been identified so quickly – 'We happened to have a student worker who played volleyball, and she walked by the laboratory table one day, saw the plaster-cast and said, "Oh, that's an Avia." Within a day, I was on a plane up to Oregon to talk to Gerry Stubblefield, who owned the Avia shoe company at the time, and he was very kind – I was able to have shoe soles from the different sizes, so I was able to compare pattern elements.' That made Burke more confident that he could identify even fractions of a shoeprint, but the news he brought back from the marketing department at Avia was at least as useful.

Only 1,354 pairs of that precise model of aerobic shoe had been made. Of those, only six had been sold on the West Coast. And of those, just one single pair had been size eleven-and-a-half. So wherever that shoe left its mark, there could no longer be any doubt it was the same perpetrator. Something of an improvement on the search that had been made for any 'Richard Mena' on the criminal files – there turned out to be 40, all of whom had to be checked, although it was in any case going to prove to be an alias.

As the news came in that the bloody footprint on Ma Bell's clock had indeed turned out to be that distinctive Avia, Salerno and Carillo got another call. 'Friday, 28 June, at about ten o'clock in the morning', recalls Carillo, 'I got notified that I'm getting a murder with Frank. This was actually the first case I got to work with Frank as a partner, not a subordinate, so off we go to Arcadia, which is in the East San Gabriel Valley again, and Arcadia is a city which has its own police department, but we do their homicide investigations. We found the body of Patty Elaine Higgins, a schoolteacher in her late 20s. She was in the bathroom; her clothes had been removed; there was blunt force trauma; her throat had been cut; it appeared she had been sexually assaulted; the house had been ransacked.'

No gunshot, no footprint – and Patty's duplex was next door to a building site, from where a bar had been taken to break into her house. The two detectives could not assume it was the Nightstalker – it could have been a worker from the site. But while they were making all the routine enquiries in the neighbourhood the two men got another call, once more to Arcadia, scarcely a mile from Patty Higgins' home.

'It was a hot day – a really hot day – and I was really tired; I was miserable out there', says Carillo. Mary Louise Cannon, an elderly widow, lived alone. Salerno and Carillo could quickly see that entry had been achieved by wrenching off the screen on an open window – for all the growing panic, if Californians claim it's hot, it really is hot. 'We went in, and observed right away that Mary Cannon had suffered blunt force trauma; her throat had been severely cut, and it looked like her hands had been ligatured in some fashion. In the bedroom, we could see that the nap on the new carpeting there was depressed, and there were shoe-prints in it.'

By now, this was a clue of almost overriding interest. Criminalist Giselle LaVigne went out to the scene to super-vize a trainee in her department, 'and did something that I had never seen done before. We actually cut out the carpet where the impression was found and took it back to the lab for additional photography.' Carillo recalls that, for safety, 'we taped it on to a piece of wood that we found.' It was, of course, that same careless signature of the Nightstalker, who had yet again found an extra method of inflicting his murderous rage. Mary Cannon had been beaten with a heavy glass vase which had been beside her bed, and whose bloodstained shards were all over the carpet she had only just had installed.

Even the most sceptical investigators now accepted that there was a peculiarly menacing serial killer on the loose. Salerno, whose Hillside Strangler investigation had convinced him that 'investigation by committee doesn't work' wasn't too happy about it, but the public, media and political pressures were now such that his rather informal squad was beefed up to a full-blown task force. What's more, the media trumpeted the news, so that the Nightstalker now knew that his various crimes were being linked and that he had a veritable posse of detectives on his trail. If anything, it appears to have excited to him even more frenetic activity.

Obsessional as the Sheriff's Office had become about their serial killer, life – and crime – still went on around them. On the afternoon of 4 July, when Salerno and Carillo were working the swing shift, in theory from 2 pm until 10 pm, they got a completely unrelated call. 'They had a stabbing murder inside the jail, so we have to go and help, and get home probably about three o'clock, three-thirty in the morning – and within half an hour get notified there's another attempted murder in Sierra Madre, and they're requesting assistance. I start to laugh, because I can't cry, and by this time my family is only living at home part-time, because I'm not home much. I remember the office asking if I wanted them to call Frank or would I do it, and I told them I would, because Frank has a temper sometimes. He wasn't happy at all – said he was tired – but I just told him the address and said I'd see him there.'

They arrived at the home of 16-year-old Whitney Bennett. Her father had woken up to the sounds of moaning and went to check: he walked into his daughter's bedroom and saw Whitney, in Carillo's words, 'a bloody pulp; unconscious; she'd suffered 42 inches of laceration to her head, she had skull fractures, a fractured jaw and cheek-bone, a fractured arm and rib, had ligature strangulation marks around her neck – he had left her for dead.'

Whitney was rushed off to hospital where, miraculously, they managed to save her life (she was eventually to marry one of the Sheriff's deputies) and the following morning the team began combing the house, the garden and Whitney's bedroom in particular for clues. Gil recalls it as being 1.40 in the afternoon when Giselle LaVigne emerged from the girl's room and said, 'Excuse me, fellas; there's something in here I'd like to show you.' What Giselle had found, beside the bed, was another bloodstained footprint: and by now everyone could recognize the Avia ridge-marks as soon as they saw them. So, despite the fact that yet another novel weapon – a tyre-iron – had been used, and that Whitney had not, apparently, been sexually assaulted, no doubts were seriously expressed. In fact, as Giselle reports, 'I was told that any further crime scenes that were even similar I would be called out to.'

Salerno's squad had meanwhile been trawling through the records of every known sex-criminal, and recent sex-crime, in the county, and finally picked up on Carol Kyle, whom Burbank had not, of course, brought to their attention earlier. Detectives were despatched to interview her, and not only did her description fit the bill – dressed all in black, malodorous, insistent that she swore an oath on Satan, and Hispanic – but she told them she'd not been really happy with the Burbank composite. They brought in their own artist to try another – and this one not only satisfied Carol, but bore a close resemblance to the very first, based on Maria Hernandez's description.

Two days later, the Nightstalker returned to Monterey Park. If he thought he was taking a risk, he didn't appreciate quite how much, nor the freaks of coincidence that can happen. On the night he'd murdered Bill Doi, a newspaper deliverywoman called Launie Dempster had noticed him and thought there was something odd, although nothing odd enough to call 911. This time, her attention was caught once more – but again, a vague feeling of unease isn't quite enough to justify calling the cops. So she continued on her round, and the killer selected the home of 61-year-old divorcée Joyce Nelson. He made his customary skilful entry, and the first Joyce can have known of him was to wake from her doze on the couch to see him standing over her pointing his .22 pistol. Just like Maxine Zazzara and Ma Bell, Joyce Nelson offered him spirited resistance – so, instead of shooting her, this time he punched, kicked and stabbed her to death.

Giselle LaVigne hadn't quite realized what her new assignment on 5 July might involve. 'Little did I know that, two days later, there would be another one – Joyce Nelson. We found a shoe impression that was the Avia on her back porch, and that linked another case to the series.' As did, after autopsy, the identical impression on Joyce's brutally-battered face. But Joyce wasn't even discovered until after the marauder had struck again.

Not for the first time, a single monstrous irruption into an innocent stranger's life seemed not to have been enough for a night's work. By 3 am on 8 June the Nightstalker was back in Monterey Park, this time outside the house of 63-year-old Sophie Dickman, a psychiatric nurse. Yet again, he made his entry by exploiting the pet-door at the rear, and eased his way into Sophie's bedroom, flashlight in one hand, pistol in the other. As she awoke, he threatened her in obscene language and locked her wrists in handcuffs. Sophie immediately realized who the intruder must be, and equally quickly worked out that her only chance of survival was to draw as deeply as she could on her lifetime's professional experience. Although he beat, raped and sodomized her and stole what few items of jewellery she had, he did not kill her.

After he had left, Sophie struggled over to the window. She knew that her neighbour across the street, Linda Arthur,was actually a Sheriff's deputy herself (indeed, Linda's husband, a colleague in the department, had recently been murdered in the course of duty) so she yelled as loud as she could until Linda was awoken. She dashed across the street, heard from Sophie what had happened and as quickly returned home to ring the emergency number. Then she rang her own office and asked them to rouse Carillo and get him to telephone her at home. She had a very strong suspicion that this was yet another addition to his workload.

Gil was at home, although his family no longer were: they'd sought refuge with his wife's parents. Not only was he at home, but thoroughly awake, having had a nightmare that the Nightstalker was actually inside his own house. As soon as he got the call he rang Linda Arthur, who told him of Sophie's rape, and her suspicions.

His memory is that 'I didn't bother to ring up Frank Salerno, because I didn't know if this case was related, I didn't know if Linda was getting emotionally involved because her husband had been murdered, so I got dressed and went to Linda's house, right across the street from where Sophie Dickman was raped. It wasn't an official call from my department – Monterey Park didn't request me, a colleague did – so I just stood out there across the street with Linda when a sergeant from Monterey Park came up, and he wasn't as nice as the guy outside the Dois: he was very profane – said "What the f-word are you doing here?" I looked at him, said "Good morning, nice to see ya, I'm here because a friend of mine called me to come and visit, and she just happens to be your informant, but she is my friend, and the last I checked, I can still come and see friends; but now that you have my attention, whenever you are done processing your crime scene I 'd like to take a look at it." And the Captain from Monterey Park Police came and said I could look at it right now.'

Having looked at Sophie's house, Carillo called his wife at her mother's house and invited them all out to breakfast. At about ten in the morning, they all went back to Gil's in-laws' home in Pica Rivera, and, as he says, 'I asked my wife to give me an hour's sleep, because I had to go back to work at noon. She said, "Gil, you can't keep going at this pace: you're going to kill yourself", and I said, "I've got to keep going – I've got a case", and just then my bleeper went off again – "Get back to Monterey Park; we've found another victim." Joyce Nelson. The press shows up to this residence, they see Frank and myself, they're saying "No more Mr Nice Guys", and the frenzy is on. It was getting kind of tough.'

Funnily enough, Carillo was also feeling curiously better. 'Now, I've got homicide investigators to believe me. They are believing one person could be responsible for this. People had thought I was essentially full of hot air. Think about it: nobody in criminal history had done, or been caught doing, what I was alleging.' And, after all the slights he'd had to bear, 'That was the first time that Monterey Park finally acknowledged that, hey, there is something going on here.'

The growing army of investigators began fanning out to check every pawnshop in the county and its cities for the items stolen from the various victims. Shoeshops were being subjected to an even more intense survey. That kind of procedural, wearisome detection has to be done, takes time and offers no guarantee of success. But at least the killer gave them a fortnight to get on with it.

Then, on 20 July, he ran amok once more. Unquestionably without premeditation, he added to the task force's bureaucratic and diplomatic burdens by striking on a single night in yet two more jurisdictions – Sun Valley and Glendale, of which Frank Salerno had fairly jaundiced memories from the Hillside killings.

Although no one was any longer musing about some

special animus towards South-east Asians – only the killer's proficiency with weapons suggested he might have served in Vietnam – the first family he destroyed that night was from Thailand. The second were Americans for several genera-tions, but of European descent. One family was young, the other old. In one, the primary weapon was a pistol; in the other, yet another innovation in horror – a machete. But such variations in MO no longer fazed the investigators: these were the all-too-familiar onslaughts of the Nightstalker.

The first call to Gil Carillo came from Scott Carrier in the County Coroner's Office – whoever else the different police forces chose to keep in the dark, they were legally obliged to notify the Coroner the moment they found a body. Carrier said 'Hey, Gil; I was out at a house in Glendale, and then there's one that happened in the LAPD's area in Sun Valley, and I think it looks like what you guys are working on, so I tried to get them to contact you, but they didn't believe it.'

Suppressing his frustrated sighs, Carillo rang John Perkins in Glendale and established that their case involved the murders of Max and Linda Kneiding, by gunshot and machete. When he arrived to view the scene – 'There was a great amount of blood-spattering up and down the walls, so somebody had really done a number there' – a couple of LAPD officers also arrived, because of the murder in their area. Carillo seized the opportunity to invite himself back with them to their scene in Sun Valley. 'When we walked up to theirs I said, "It's him", because there was a footprint, as clear as day.'

What's more, there was another survivor. Thai immigrant Chainrong Khovananth had been shot in the head before the intruder bound his wife, Somkid, with electrical cord and then raped and sodomized her.

All the while their two young children were in the house, and Carillo discovered that when the first officers arrived at the scene, their eight-year old boy was lying, bound and naked, on his face – 'They found baby oil where there had been an attempted sexual assault on him' – the final proof that Carillo had been right all along: this offender really was the first in the annals of crime to combine paedophilia with adult rape, burglary and murder.

Somkid gave her description, which certainly didn't surprise anyone on the Task Force: tall, dark-skinned, thirty-ish, bad teeth – oh, and he'd made her swear to Satan that she'd given him all the money and jewellery she had.

Although there were now dozens of detectives seconded to the task force, Salerno's engrained lack of confidence in investigation by committee meant that he and Gil were working seven days a week, and well beyond their theoretical shift-times. The media were being kept off their backs as best the Sheriff's Office could manage but, hard as the team toiled, they still lacked a truly positive lead. On the other hand, among the killer's criminal acquaintances – not least his regular fence – there was a growing suspicion, and an associated fear.

On 5 August, having stolen yet another Toyota (not so much a brand preference as that he had a master key to the model), the killer turned his attention to Northridge, 25 miles from downtown LA. There, at around 2 am, he picked out the home of Chris and Virginia Petersen. He broke in, strode into the bedroom and shot both with his latest gun, a .25 automatic. But Chris, a big, strapping man of 38 who worked in a warehouse, couldn't be stopped by a single small-calibre bullet which had, for once, hit the temple rather than the dead-centre of his forehead. He lunged at the Nightstalker and grappled with him. More shots were fired in the melée, but they missed – and suddenly the intruder realized his gun was empty. Breaking loose, he fled back to his car, and to LA.

Both the Petersens – and their children – survived. There were no tell-tale shoe-prints, but the description the victims gave was enough to suggest this one, too, should be added to the list.

That morning, Salerno had called a meeting of all the involved police forces in the county – representatives attended at the LAPD from Arcadia, Burbank, Glendale, Monrovia, Montebello, Monterey Park, Sierra Madre, West Covina and the FBI. Salerno's message was blunt – the Nightstalker was blatantly exploiting all their territorial distinctions, and if they didn't pool all information they wouldn't win.

Carillo's family were still staying at his in-laws' house, but on the night of 8 August they came home for dinner and to stay over. At 4.30 in the morning Gil's police radio, which he kept beside his bed, carried a call for him to ring in. 'I said, "OK, right", and my wife said. "Where are you going this time?" and I said, "Diamond Bar", which is right next to where I live.' He went off, but when he returned his wife said she was leaving, and that she and the kids would not be back until the case was all over. 'She didn't even take time to put anything in luggage', he reports. 'She just got brown paper bags, threw a bunch of clothes in and said, "That's it."'

The Diamond Bar intrusion to which Carillo had been called was at the home of another couple of immigrants from Asia – Pakistani Elyas Abowath and his Burmese wife, Sakina. Elyas had been shot dead, Sakina raped, sodomized and beaten, their three-year old son tied up. The nature of the crime was by now enough to identify the Nightstalker, but Sakina's description confirmed it: tall, dressed in black, bad teeth – and insistent that she swore to Satan there was nothing else of value in the house after he had ransacked it. But Sakina, a doctor, could add one more identifying clue: she had somehow managed to note that her assailant was uncircumcised.

What Carillo immediately spotted was a footprint. This time, it wasn't the familiar Avia at all, but it was the same large size. The detective says, 'He had changed shoes – but we knew it was the same person.'

The killer did not, of course, know that it was his feet that were giving him away, not his carefully-gloved fingers. That information had been scrupulously kept from the media, who were by now carrying reams of hysterical speculation every day. What he did know was that things were getting hot in Los Angeles County, where every force seemed at last to have conceded that they had a common nightmare. So he decided his next strike should take place far to the north, in San Francisco. Given the distance, he treated himself to a little extra comfort, and stole a Mercedes-Benz.

Fortunately, the San Francisco Police displayed a faster learning curve than had Monterey Park. When they were called to the home of a Taiwanese couple, Peter and Barbara Pan, to discover 66-year-old Peter shot dead and 62-year-old Barbara raped and beaten, their assailant having drawn pentagrams on the wall, they made an instant connection with the cases they had been reading about in Los Angeles and got in touch. Carillo and Salerno flew up – Gil says 'with a sigh of relief: "He's not down here, he's up there"' – and exchanged information with the local cops. But if their professional colleagues were helpful, no allowance had been made for the irresponsibility of ambitious politicians.

The then-Mayor of San Francisco was Dianne Feinstein, later to become Senator Feinstein. She summoned a press conference at City Hall, not just to announce that the Nightstalker was now threatening her city, but to give detailed information on how the connection had been made. To the horrified fury of Salerno and Carillo, she told the world about the Avia shoes, and all the ballistic evidence linking both the .22 and the .25.

The killer ought to have been grateful to San Francisco, not just for tipping him off but for providing, with the Golden Gate Bridge, the ideal place for throwing old shoes into oblivion. But once he'd done that, the charms of the city palled – so, still driving the stolen Merc, he went south once more.

What Dianne Feinstein fortunately did not know – to be fair, nobody did – was that one of the killer's cronies was undergoing a crisis, almost certainly of fear rather than conscience. Jesse Perez had more than enough previous form to feel apprehensive about approaching any policeman directly, but he confided his growing suspicions about an oddball burglar he knew called Rick to his daughter, whose family upbringing had taught her to think long and hard about playing the good citizen. She took her time before seeking a lawyer's advice as to the best course – after all, as her father had told her that Rick had strongly hinted he'd murdered in the course of some of his burglaries, that might expose Jesse himself to charges.

Meanwhile, the Nightstalker – let's now call him Rick – decided to switch his attention further south again. Mission Viejo is 60-odd miles south of LA, and in the wealthiest county of the State, Orange County. Rick dumped the Mercedes (which not one single traffic cop or state trooper had spotted in the week he had driven it up and down California) and reverted to the easy route. This time, the Toyota was an orange-coloured station wagon: not necessarily the vehicle of choice in Mission Viejo, however popular it might be in South Central LA.

At about one o'clock on the morning of 25 August, Rick switched off the lights on the car and cruised slowly down Chrisanta Drive. On his feet, not the Avias any longer, but exactly the same shoes he'd worn when he murdered Elyas Abowath. While he was hunting for a suitable target, he was quite unaware that his curious unlit progress had caught the attention of a teenage boy who was tinkering with his motor-scooter in a neighbouring driveway. James Romero thought it odd, but no more than that.

Rick picked upon the home of William and Carole Cairns. Bill Cairns was one of California's new elite – a computer expert. Their house may have been expensive, but it was just as easy to break into as any other, and the Nightstalker prised away the screen from a back window before slipping silently in. He made his way to the master bedroom and, as Bill woke, shot him three times in the head. Carole's terror was compounded by the fact that the intruder this time actu-ally announced himself as the Nightstalker before binding her, looting the house and then returning to rape and sodomize her, exact the familiar oath to Satan and depart.

But as he sped by, James Romero was still working on his bike, and was again puzzled by the orange Toyota and its black-clad driver. This time, he tried to take a note of its licence-plate, getting three digits down.

Suddenly, Rick's luck began to run out at speed. The long-drawn-out ordeal from June 1984 to August 1985 almost raced to a conclusion in the last week of the latter month. As soon as James Romero heard about the Cairns murder he told his parents, who told the Orange County Sheriff's Office: which meant that when the orange Toyota was found three days later, it was instantly identified as a suspect vehicle and given the full treatment. It had been wiped down – save only for a single fingerprint where Rick had adjusted the rear-view mirror.

Jesse Perez's daughter had finally contacted Salerno and Carillo the day before. She told them what her father had said about the drifter called Rick, and asked for protection for him, which was immediately offered. Jesse offered a range of additional clues. Rick was a burglar, and his regular fence was a man called Felipe Solano. Rick talked about Satan a lot, and came from El Paso. He'd once sold Jesse a .22, which Jesse had then given to a female friend down in Tijuana. And Rick had been arrested late in 1984 for stealing a car and then crashing into a bus terminal when trying to evade police pursuit.

Up in San Francisco, investigators had got similarly lucky – well, as Gary Player once said, the more you practice, the luckier you get – when they let the media have pictures of the jewellery stolen from the Pans. A woman in Lompoc (which just happens to have a Federal pentitentiary as one of its more prominent local industries) recognized a gift she'd been given by a friend. The friend was a friend of a burglar called Rick, a man who was keen on both Satan and the group AC/DC. He came from El Paso

San Francisco pressed on, tracking the connections until they reached another drifter in the chain, Armando Rodriguez. Although at first he refused to speak to the cops, the suggestion that the next charge on his sheet could be one of accessory after the fact to murder mysteriously coaxed out of him the fact that Rick's last name was Ramirez.

The first computer check into California's criminal records revealed that rather a lot of Rick, Richard and Ricardo Ramirez's had form: running into the thousands, in fact.

But, thanks to the orange Toyota, there was now a means of pruning the list. As Carillo recalls, 'They matched it to just one Richard Ramirez – who'd been arrested for Grand Theft Auto in Los Angeles, did time, and we got pictures.'

The pictures were shown to Jesse Perez. 'That's him', he said. A search of Felipe Solano's garage had turned up all manner of stolen goods, but those of greatest interest could all be tied to a Nightstalker incident. Things were finally falling into place.

Dianne Feinstein wasn't the only one whose judgment was heavily influenced by the next election. Sheriff Block of Los Angeles County knew his job depended on getting the Nightstalker, and after consulting similarly career-conscious senior colleagues in other jurisdictions he decided that the mugshot and name of Richard Muñoz Ramirez should be made public.

Salerno and Carillo weren't happy. They pointed out that releasing the name and picture would give Ramirez very public warning to skip town and disappear. On the other hand, not doing so would leave him free to strike again.

On 30 August, every newspaper and TV station in the state carried both name and picture. What the cops thought was that Ramirez would make a run for it – try to get out of LA as fast as he could. So, as Carillo says, 'We had cops all around the bus station: we expected him to come walking up to the building. What we didn't know was he was on a bus coming back from Arizona the morning of the 31st.' Ramirez had been down to visit his brother Robert in

Tucson. Robert didn't know about Richard's crimes – and, more to the point, Richard didn't know what was all over the California media. He rode back into a city, a county and a state where every eye was alert for the Nightstalker, but the Nightstalker was himself quite unaware his anonymity was lost.

Carillo picks up the story. 'When he exited the bus, he went walking through the terminal and he noticed there were too many cops around – there was something going on – so he went out the back way, went into a local liquor store and then saw his picture on the front page of the paper. He jumped on a local bus, just trying to make it out of Los Angeles, but somebody on the bus identified him, looked at him, looked at their paper – very obvious – pulled the cord, exited the bus and went right to a phone booth, and Richard could see him making the 911 call. So Richard stayed on the bus for another half-mile, exited and started running. He ran across a major freeway, went over a ten-foot wall and was in the process of trying to steal a car when a husband heard his wife screaming, ran out to save her, grabbed a piece of pipe and hit Richard in the head a couple of times.

Richard was by now exhausted from about a two-mile sprint over hill and dale, and then getting hit by a pipe, and only made it about another 15, 20 yards down the street, because by now the neighbours were coming out and chasing him, and he finally just gave up and sat on a kerb, and started saying, "It's me". They really didn't know who they had, and nor did the first arriving member of the County

Sheriff's department, a rookie cop also called Ramirez. All he knew was he was arresting someone who was trying to steal a car. He had him handcuffed on the back seat of the car, called the paramedics, and while he was still taking down information the boys in blue, our colleagues the Los Angeles Police Department, whose jurisdiction was less than half a block away, pulled up and a sergeant said that was the guy they'd been chasing, instructed his men to take him out of the car, and before Andy Ramirez could do anything they'd taken him out of the car and were transporting him to their own Hollenbeck station.'

So much for Salerno's stern message about co-operation, not competition. Still, the key thing was that Richard Ramirez was no longer at liberty. Carillo admits he felt ambivalent. 'I wanted to get inside his brain, you know? I'd spent so much of my life, and it impacted on my life so much. I had so many unanswered questions: the other side of me was hoping that somebody had taken his life, saved me an awful lot of stress and saved the county taxpayers an awful lot of money.'

After that culminating, giddy, exhilarating week, of course, the story slowed down to the customary funereal pace of California justice. Charged with 14 murders, 22 sexual assaults and 32 other felonies on 29 September 1985, Ramirez eventually went to trial on 29 January 1989. On 20 September 1989, he was found guilty of 13 murders and 30 felonies, and sentenced to the gas chamber.

He's still busy exhausting the interminable appeals

system. Oh – and in October 1996, on Death Row, he got married to a magazine writer called Doreen Loiy. I think the only possible reaction has to be, 'Go figure'.

ERIK AND LYLE MENENDEZ

When the door to the family room was opened a little after ten o'clock on the evening of Sunday, 20 August 1989, it seems almost certain that both José and Kitty Menendez were dozing in front of the TV. They'd been out until midnight on Saturday, shark-fishing, and the remains of their light supper were still in the room.

Within the next few seconds, the two men who had slipped so quietly into the house had fired six shells each from the automatic shotguns they carried, and José was dead, Kitty dying. To make entirely sure, the killers dashed out of the house, reloaded their guns and went back to finish Kitty off. The white-painted room was spattered with blood and fragments of flesh.

Not the kind of thing that normally happens in Beverley Hills, and especially not in ultra-expensive and exclusive Elm Drive. After all, the Menendez house had not only cost

ERIK AND LYLE MENENDEZ

them $3.5 million the year before, but it had the state-of-the-art security systems you might expect of a property which had in the past been rented to tenants such as Prince and Elton John.

The call to Detective Les Zoeller came at about 11.45 pm. '20 August', he recalls, 'was actually the next to last day of my vacation, so I was in bed when my boss came on the phone and said he had a double murder. I said "I'm still on vacation" and he said, "You were on vacation."'

Now, as Zoeller says, 'The city of Beverley Hills doesn't have that many homicides – they average two a year – so from 1980 to 1989 I probably worked only eight to ten murders', which still made him one of the most experienced cops in the Detective division there. As he dressed and then drove to the police station, running through his mind was the thought that 'unless there's a break-in, the victims knew the suspects.'

When he and his colleague arrived at the Menendez house, already cordoned off by uniformed officers, he was hit by 'one of the worst crime scenes I had ever seen. They had a big-screen television, and it was still on. There was some blood splatter on the screen. The man was sitting on the couch, with his head tilted to the right, and we could see between the couch and the coffee table a female, and she was just covered in blood. There were body parts on the ceiling, there was a shotgun blast that had gone through the French door to the yard. My initial thought was, "Oh, my God, what a mess." I had never known a scene like it.'

Under California law, the police may not touch a body but

must await the Coroner. Even so, lying as the two corpses were, it was clear to Zoeller that 'Mr Menendez was shot in the back of the head with a shotgun, it looked like he was shot in the chest area and on his leg, and Mrs Menendez had a shot in her leg, a shotgun blast to the side of her face. They had both been hit numerous times – we hadn't counted, because we couldn't get a full look. I had never seen a sight like that before.'

Despite their horror, the detectives went about their business. 'We collected as much evidence as we could', says Zoeller, 'fingerprints, hair and so forth, and then we went in to interview the witnesses.'

Two vital witnesses were José and Kitty's sons, Lyle and Erik. The two boys – 21-year old Lyle, a university student, 18-year old Erik, just finishing school – had been out for the evening, had returned home, and first discovered the carnage.

Lyle had made the call to the emergency services number, 911, at 11.47 pm. 'We're the sons' he began, and then broke down. The operator asked him what the problem was, and Lyle began again 'My parents...' and then, prompted once again, managed to stutter, 'Shot and killed.'

When the first uniformed police responded to the call, the two young men ran out of the house to greet them, screaming and sobbing. In case the killers might still be in the house, the officers told the boys to remain outside and went in to confront the scene. As they searched the house, they discovered in Kitty's bedroom both her dog, Rudy, and two unfired .22 rifles which she kept for security.

A canvass of the neighbours revealed that nobody had heard Rudy barking, and that those who had heard the noise of the fatal shots had written them off as firecrackers. One man remarked that he didn't think it could be gunfire, 'especially around here. It was just pops – these houses are quite solid, and it really didn't sound that impressive.'

Nevertheless, one local girl did recollect seeing a small white hatchback stopping near the house at around 10pm. Two men, she said, had got out, taken something from the back and walked towards the house.

Lyle and Erik had been driven to the police station, where Sergeant Tom Edmunds tried to coax more details out of them. As he relayed to Zoeller, 'they were saying that their father was in a business that had some kind of sketchy Mafia overtones.'

Not much to go on, but the police were in any case committed to finding out as much as they could about the family background. And, as the Elm Drive mansion and the Mercedes 560 SEL in the drive would suggest, they quickly discovered that 45-year old José was an all-American success story: a refugee from Castro's Cuba who had captured the campus beauty queen at Southern Illinois University, and whose subsequent business career had been so noteworthy that his murder made the front page of the *Wall Street Journal*.

He'd qualified as an accountant, then risen meteorically through the Hertz car rental company to the top of their United States domestic leasing business: then on to RCA

Records in New York, where he'd done deals with Scotland's superstar Annie Lennox and relaunched Jefferson Starship; and, most recently, to California, where he'd transformed the fortunes of a video distribution business, International Video Entertainment. Before José took over, the company had been deeply in the red. Within one year, he'd steered it back into the black. After three years, IVE's revenues had risen from $40 million a year to $400 million, and José's annual bonus had hit $1 million.

It did emerge, however, that José hadn't got to the top by playing Mr. Nice Guy. One of his former colleagues at Hertz called the Beverley Hills police to ask them why they hadn't contacted him, or any of the other victims of the arrogant and bullying Menendez management style: for, as he said, 'I would have done the job for nothing but, at the least, I wanted to shake the hand of the actual killers.' Indeed, the office joke within the car rental giant after the murder was to call colleagues and demand to know if they had an alibi for 20 August.

District Attorney Pam Boznavich recollects that it was 'very difficult to find anyone who would come forward and say anything good about José Menendez: in fact, the only one who did was his secretary.'

Nevertheless, another of the ruthless José's achievements had been to take over other companies and turn International Video Entertainment into LIVE Entertainment, and in the course of that, he had indeed given apparent provocation to two men allegedly linked to organized crime. Les Zoeller, like most professional detectives, says he hates 'to use the name Mafia', but given what the sons had told Sergeant Edmunds, the possibility of Mob involvement had to be explored. Indeed, in popular legend, it was widely, if erroneously, held that the shooting of both José and Kitty in the knee was a kind of Mafia signature on the killings. (As far as I can discover, there is no substance to this at all. 'Kneecapping' is part of the peculiar disciplinary culture of Northern Ireland, and in America the most common trademark of the Mob is the use of small-calibre pistols rather than shotguns. However...)

The first name into the frame was that of Morris Levy. José Menendez had bought a large chain of record retailers from Levy at, it was said, an arm-twistingly low price, since Levy was badly strapped for cash. Why? Because he had been fighting a lengthy and expensive court battle against the FBI on charges of extortion (he'd lost – and got ten years) and had been described in court as an associate of Vincente 'The Chin' Gigante, reputed boss of the Genovese crime family. But inquiries showed that Levy and Menendez had never met during the negotiations, and that the price LIVE paid, $40.5 million, was neither outrageously low nor, probably, over the top. One conspiracy down, but still one to go.

Noel Bloom always looked a better bet. His father had been in the top-shelf magazine business – what were styled in Fifties America as 'Nudie Cuties' and by Lenny Bruce 'stroke mags', and son Noel's brilliant insight had been to see that home video players opened a huge market for pornographic movies. Noel began by converting existing dirty pictures on to video, and progressed to making his own original cheap-and-nasties for rental. As the money flowed in (one Bloom office had a jacuzzi big enough for ten), organized crime undoubtedly took an interest, and demanded one. According to one investigation, the booming blue video industry, not just Bloom's enterprise, was by 1980 making pay-offs to the Gambino, Galante, DeCavalcante and Colombo crime families. And the US Department of Justice alleged that Bloom himself was 'an associate' of Michael Zaffarano, in turn alleged to be the Galante family's California boss.

Bloom's business had got into trouble in the mid-80s because he wanted to branch out from pornography, and into the renting of respectable movies. He quickly found out that there was an enormous gulf between low-budget smut and mainstream Hollywood product. One consequence was that he had to sell a slice of his operation for a $25 million line of credit – and the purchasers insisted on bringing in a financial manager. That was Menendez, who proceeded to slash the staff from 500 to 175, much to Bloom's disgust. He soon concluded that Menendez was determined to drive him out completely, so agreed to sell the remainder of his stock for a rumoured $1.4 million.

He'd lost his company but, even worse, the final half-million dollars of his pay-off didn't arrive. Bloom sued, and Menendez gave savage testimony which humiliated and infuriated Bloom. A possible motive – but it didn't seem to get the police excited. They didn't even get around to interviewing Bloom until a fortnight after the deaths and, to his own surprise, didn't even ask him to account for his movements on the night of 20 August.

That was because, by then, other suspicions were rising to the surface. After the autopsies, which revealed just how many shots had hit the couple, Les Zoeller concluded: 'It was definitely an overkill – more anger than revenge or any other motive.' And he had also begun to think that 'there was something about the brothers which just didn't set right with us. The morning after the deaths we were still at the crime scene, and the officers that were protecting it from outside came to us and said the sons were here; they want to pick up some stuff. The Coroner had just got there, so I said, "Well, have the boys come back in a couple of hours", thinking that they were going to stay somewhere else and just want to get some fresh clothes.

'After a few hours passed the same officer came in and said the brothers were back, so I went out to speak to Lyle and asked what kind of stuff did he want to get, and he said, "Well, we're staying at our tennis coach's house, and we want to get tennis gear that's in the room where the murder occurred." I think my jaw dropped to the floor. I just couldn't believe that, so that stuck in my mind as this uncaring son; you know, he found his parents shot to death in this family room and here he is, all he can think about is getting his tennis gear out because he's staying with his tennis coach. That stuck in the back of my mind.'

Others had also begun to wonder about the boys. One of José and Kitty's friends was called Pete Wiere. Zoeller went to see him and asked what his initial reaction had been when he heard about the murders. Wiere's immediate response surprised both men. 'I have no basis for this', he said, 'but I wonder if the boys did it.' Zoeller asked him to explain, and Wiere couldn't really offer anything concrete – just an emotional feeling that Lyle and Erik were not quite the tennis-playing, well-mannered, devoted sons they seemed.

Zoeller also noted the curious demeanour of the boys at the memorial service held in Hollywood for their parents. 'They came, like, an hour late; they came in a limousine; they came impeccably dressed like they were the stars of the show – it just wasn't right. They had gotten, initially, hundreds of thousands of dollars, and they were spending it like water. It turned out that before the memorial service they had gone into Century City and bought Rolex watches and expensive suits and money clips and so on – I mean, they just weren't acting like innocent sons or that their parents had been murdered.'

Intuition is not, of course, admissible evidence in court, and a month after the killings Zoeller really didn't have much more than a hunch to go on. In mid-September he went three thousand miles east to interview the boys' uncle and aunt in New Jersey. He told them he was irritated that Erik and Lyle hadn't been returning his calls, and he still hadn't really been able to talk to them, at which point Mrs Terry Baralt, José's sister, told him that Erik was upstairs at that very moment and she would fetch him down. As she did so, a car drew up outside to reveal Lyle was also visiting. Zoeller

ERIK AND LYLE MENENDEZ

took the chance to ask the brothers if their parents often dozed off in front of the television, and Lyle told him it was very common for his father, much less so for his mother, but that she might well have been exhausted from the previous evening's fishing trip.

Zoeller then told them of his growing theory that their parents had known their killers, because there were no signs that either of them had struggled (and, as the crime scene report had noted, there were no signs of a break-in). Lyle and Erik merely replied that their mother had grown increasingly worried about security, buying the rifles and making a fuss about locking the doors, and when Zoeller asked if there had been any trouble between them and their parents, volunteered that there had been an argument the day before the killings over exactly that – Kitty's insistence on locking up, and Lyle's offhand attitude to the subject.

The press were, of course, taking a big interest in the case. The slaughter of a senior Hollywood executive and his wife in such an exclusive, expensive, and security-conscious area was a major story in a city where murder is commonplace, but normally confined to the anonymous poor. The *Los Angeles Times* put two reporters on the story to the exclusion of everything else. Ron Soble and John Johnson were both experienced men, and although they too began by checking out the Mob-hit theory, they made no more progress on it than had the police. Indeed, when they spoke to Bloom, he almost charmed them.

So they, too, sought an interview with the sons. The line they had planned to take was very much a human-interest slant – 'a portrait of two young men suddenly thrust out on their own in a horrifically brutal way. How were they bearing up under the weight of their loss?' They were invited up to Elm Drive, and almost immediately thrown by the unemotional attitude the boys took. Lyle's opening remark to the newsmen was: 'If the focus of the story is the investigation, really, I want no part of it, because I'm really tired of this investigation.'

As the conversation went on, Lyle managed to convey the impression that he didn't really care if the case was solved, but that it was his firm belief that the Mob, and specifically Bloom, had ordered the hit. He then revealed that both of them now planned to use their inheritance to fund attempts to establish themselves in professional tennis.

When the two reporters returned to their waiting car, both feeling stunned by the ice-cold attitudes they had encountered, they exchanged glances before Soble spoke. 'They did it', he said.

If juries were empanelled from experienced cops and reporters, the case was almost closed. But since they're not, there wasn't even the beginnings of a case to bring. Zoeller had to go on digging. It wasn't even much comfort that when he took the whole problem to two colleagues who had been through the FBI's 'profiling' course, which assesses any given crime against the historic record of similar offences and suggests the probable personality of the perpetrator, they said, 'We agree with you: Erik and Lyle are the people to look at.'

The hunch, if not the evidence, continued to get support.

Zoeller was slightly thrown by the fact that 'when Erik was on the West Coast, Lyle was on the East Coast: when Lyle was on the West Coast, it turned out that Erik was on the East Coast. I mean, we just couldn't keep tabs on these boys. And at one point Lyle had come in to Beverley Hills, and we learned that he had hired a computer expert, and we discovered that he was concerned that his parents were going to take Erik and himself out of their will, so he hired this expert to come and look over the computer files and told him: 'I want you to make it look like nobody ever looked at it' – and this guy read the computer, which had nothing in it, but erased the files he couldn't read.'

That was already late October – ten weeks into the investigation – but that piece of non-evidence was to provoke the first real break in the brothers' disciplined defence. As Zoeller tells it, 'we found out that the press had also found out about this computer expert and were going to report it, so we went up to the Menendez residence, where we believed both Erik and Lyle were staying, and when we knocked on the door Erik answered. So we told Erik about the computer, and said that it didn't look good for Lyle, and that our focus was on Lyle, and said we didn't know whether Erik was involved or not, but that we were going to get to the bottom of this. So Erik of course denied everything, and said his brother was back East, and he didn't think he was involved in this – but I guess us talking to him that day shook him up enough that he went to see a psychologist that he had been to previously, a man by the name of Dr Jerome Oziel.'

Doctors – even California shrinks – share with priests and lawyers a professional obligation, and legal privilege, of confidentiality. So Dr Oziel did not pick up the phone that evening to tell Zoeller that Erik had admitted that he and Lyle had killed their parents. As Zoeller learned much later, Erik told the therapist that he couldn't live with what he had done, and was pretty much having a nervous breakdown. 'He told Oziel that they just couldn't stand their parents with the pressures they were giving.'

In other words, José's incessant demand for perfectionism – at school, in social behaviour, on the tennis courts – was the root cause which Erik had to offer on that occasion. And there was no doubt that he had indeed been a demanding parent, although it later emerged that he had been offered some severe provocations. He had given them support and protection when a series of burglaries at friends' houses had been traced to the boys, and had gone to bat for Lyle when his eldest son was given a year's suspension from Princeton for cheating in a test paper.

Oziel concluded that Lyle was the more dangerous of the two, and told Erik he would have to talk to him. The younger boy called his brother, who came right over, apparently hopping mad and, ignoring the psychologist, told Erik: 'I can't believe you did this – I don't have a brother now. You know we are going to have to do the same thing to Dr Oziel.'

It was a heated session, from which Erik fled in tears, and Oziel had the very strong impression that Lyle was threatening him and his family, which certainly reinforced his professional duty to respect patient confidence.

The police had their suspicions, but in the absence of a call from Oziel they simply plodded on checking, and eliminating, other leads. During that Fall, they looked into every aspect of José Menendez' colourful history. It was clear that he had as big a talent for making enemies as for making money, and it wasn't just at Hertz that there were people with grudges: if not enough to have killed Kitty and José, enough to volunteer information to his discredit.

Among the suggestions which Zoeller and his colleagues had to examine was that Menendez had made his real money – and the estate was being rumoured at some $14 million – by running drugs, or that Fidel Castro had ordered hit-men to take the exile out before he could pursue his stated ambition to move from business into US politics, the better to fight the Cuban regime.

It even emerged that José had had a fight with Kitty's brother over a chess game, while Erik had been in a rumble with one of Los Angeles' violent street gangs. But Zoeller was more intrigued by an interview he had with one of Erik's high school friends, Craig Cignarelli. In part, this was because one of Zoeller's earlier successes had been solving a murder arising out of a fraudulent scheme called the Billionaire Boys' Club, and Cignarelli recognized his name and volunteered that he and Erik had been fascinated by that.

Zoeller moved on to a fairly direct line of questioning. 'If Erik told you that he killed his parents', he asked, 'would you tell us?' The detective was shocked by the answer. 'He humed and ha-ed about it, and said, "I don't know what I'd do."'

But Cignarelli then went on to reveal that a couple of years earlier, he and Erik had collaborated on a story which they hoped to sell to Hollywood. 'It was a story about this wealthy family that had a son, and this son ended up killing the parents for their money. We thought that was very intriguing – very interesting – so we asked Craig for a copy of it, and we kept in touch with him, but then he got upset with our investigation and wouldn't speak to us any more, so we ended up getting a search warrant to search his house to get this play; and then, in talking to us, Craig told us that Erik had confided in him about killing his parents. He said he'd been over at the Menendez house and all of a sudden, Erik looked at him and asked if he wanted to know what happened, and Erik kind of walked him through the crime scene, but then ended up by saying, "It could have happened". Well, Craig in his own mind thought, "Well, you know Erik, he always thought about the perfect burglary, the perfect arson, the perfect murder." So he thought Erik was just testing him; just telling him another story.'

Spoilt brats who fantasize about perfect crimes aren't just the stuff of fiction, like 'Rope'; they can be brutal fact, like Leopold and Loeb, so Zoeller certainly took this new insight seriously. He persuaded Cignarelli to arrange a meeting with Erik while carrying a concealed microphone, but unfortunately 'it turned out that he met him in a restaurant in Malibu on the beach, a very, very noisy restaurant – it was a terrible connection. But he didn't admit anything, but he did enquire of Craig if he had told anybody, so it gave enough inference that he did tell him something, so all the pieces of the puzzle were being put in place, with the fingers being pointed at the brothers.'

Zoeller and his colleagues felt that Erik was the weaker of the two, very possibly being manipulated by his elder brother – one reason why the detective had fed him the story about the reporters and the computer which sent him rushing to Dr Oziel. And, during the course of the next few months, there seems to have been increasing friction between the boys: Erik talking too much to both the psychologist and his old schoolfriend, and worrying that Lyle was after the lion's share of the inheritance; Lyle concerned that his brother was capable of making an irretrievable mistake. But in fact, the really critical mistake was Dr Oziel's.

To add to his worries, the married doctor had been conducting a passionate affair with a woman called Judalon Rose Smyth who had, it seems, been in an adjoining room at the time of Erik's confession to Oziel. She both heard some of the conversation, and knew that Oziel usually taped his patients. Nevertheless, she kept the information to herself for several months, until her relationship with Oziel soured – at which point she told a friend, a lawyer, who counselled her to go to the police.

Her visit was at the beginning of March 1990, by which time the police were convinced they had the right suspects, but the District Attorney's office was equally convinced they did not have enough evidence. An exhaustive canvass of every gunshop in the area had failed to discover any purchases by the brothers, who would by law have been required to show proof of identity, and one spent shotgun cartridge which had been found by a Princeton classmate in Lyle's car had been dismissed by a ballistics expert as of the wrong type.

Smyth made the difference. As Zoeller says 'that was when we had enough to arrest the brothers.' In fact, he and the D.A. spent seven hours talking to her, all on tape, and 'with her information we had enough information for a search warrant for Oziel's home, and we got the tapes. We had to listen to the tapes to make sure we had the right ones, and we had a team watching the Menendez house, and as Lyle exited the house, he was arrested. As it turned out, Erik was in Israel at a tennis tournament. Our intention was to obtain an arrest warrant for Erik so we could get him in custody so we could transport him to California, but the family said, "No, we'll get him here", and within a day we heard that Erik was flying in to surrender, and was flying with his aunt, so we met them de-planing, and arrested Erik.'

Zoeller at that point felt confident – 'I knew it was more of a circumstantial case: we didn't have a smoking gun ' – but recognized there was still work to be done to strengthen the case. Fortunately, Smyth had told him that Erik had confided in Oziel that they had bought the shotguns at a store in San Diego, some way down the coast towards the Mexican border, and had been worried that he could be identified because the store had closed-circuit cameras.

'So now the job was to go and find out what store it was, so we went to San Diego on two separate occasions, checking gun stores.' No purchases turned up by any Menendez, and at one store which certainly did have CCTV cameras it emerged they were there purely as a deterrent, and held no film. However, two Mosbrook shotguns had been bought in that store, a branch of the Big 5 chain, in the right period of the preceding August, by a customer who identified himself by showing a driver's licence. The name leapt out at Zoeller. From all his laborious reading and re-reading of the files, he recalled that a Princeton acquaintance of Lyle's had been interviewed and complained that Lyle had stolen his driver's licence. His name was Donovan Goodreau, and he was now working at a restaurant in New York. Although he knew from the press that the brothers had been arrested, he was shaken to get a phone call from Beverley Hills soon after to be asked by Zoeller where he had been on 18 August 1989?

To his relief, and Zoeller's delight, Goodreau was able to prove from his work records that he had been thousands of miles east of San Diego on that day. DA Pam Bozanich recalls that 'during the course of the investigation, the detectives kept coming to me and saying, "Is this enough?" and I kept saying, "No, you need one piece of great physical evidence", which they did find after I was taken off the case, and that was Donovan Goodreau's drivers licence. That was the pivotal piece of evidence which put the case together.'

Bozanich was put back on the case a few months after the arrests (California justice moves at a measured pace, and the trial was not to reach court until July 1993) and made a very

ERIK AND LYLE MENENDEZ

shrewd guess about the likely defence. 'I actually told people that I thought they were going to have to use sexual abuse, because that was the only thing I could think of that they could try to get out from under, and I knew they wouldn't go for manslaughter or second-degree murder; they were going to go for the big acquittal. Now I know that Lyle Menendez told a relative that they were going to pursue this, and she said to him, "Lyle, you know that's not true", and he said to her "That's how it's going to be." I had that information before the end of the trial, but I could not put her on the stand because it would have been indecent to do so: it would have ruined her life.'

The DA proved absolutely right. The boys' defence was that José had persistently sexually abused Erik and that Kitty had abused Lyle, and that they had begun to fear for their lives. As she says, 'It was a really good story – it just wasn't true.' In fact, it now seems clear that any sexual problems in the family were caused by José's endless heterosexual infidelities to Kitty, and growing parental suspicion of Erik's homosexuality.

Les Zoeller was convinced the boys had committed the crime, and his investigations had uncovered 'absolutely no physical abuse and absolutely no sexual abuse. Mental abuse, I'll give them – José was pretty tough on the brothers.' Even so, his experience had taught him never to be confident of getting a conviction. ' Twelve people on a jury just come back sometimes with some unbelievable verdicts. You just don't know, from one case to another.'

The defence team had decided – not least after consulting the author of a book entitled *When a Child Kills: Abused Children Who Kill Their Parents*, a lawyer who believes that when a child kills, it is the parents' fault – that their best strategy was to destroy the image and reputation of the family. Despite the fact that there was no evidence that either brother had ever so much as mentioned abuse to friends or family, or indeed Dr Oziel, they committed to what Bozanich called 'a defence that is an offence.' That became quite clear when they rejected any suggestion of a plea bargain, yet told the prosecutors that the brothers would admit the killings – but show it was their parents' fault.

Erik and Lyle were indicted by the Grand Jury in December 1992, and on 14 May 1993, Judge Stanley Weissberg ruled that they should be tried together, but with two separate juries. The process of empanelling those juries, from a pool of 1,100 potential members, all of whom had to complete a 122-item questionnaire, took up yet more time, so that by the time the trial proper began, the brothers had already spent more than three years in the Los Angeles County Jail where, on at least one occasion, a guard had caught Erik in a compromising embrace with another prisoner.

The hearings took six months, the defence alone calling 56 witnesses in their studied attempt to show that Lyle and Erik had suffered physical, sexual and mental abuse, and were of the opinion that they were in 'imminent danger' from their parents.

That, under California law, would effectively mean they had acted in self-defence. It did, on the other hand, bring in the whole question of their mental state, which caused Weissberg to rule that the prosecution could call Dr Oziel to the stand to testify that no mention of the various abuses had been made when he spoke to the young men (whom the defence consistently referred to as 'children').

At the conclusion, Zoeller's cynicism proved well-placed. After 16 days of deliberation, on 13 January 1994, Erik's jury (eight men and four women) reported that it was deadlocked, with just five members voting for first-degree murder. Another eight days went by before Lyle's jury revealed that it, too, was deadlocked, with only three members voting for first-degree murder.

Judge Weissberg had no option but to declare a mistrial. The defence took the view that they had won, but the prosecution made it entirely clear that they would be going for a retrial, because, as one of the District Attorneys said, 'We would rather have a hung jury than a manslaughter verdict, because this is a murder case.'

All of this had taken its toll on Zoeller, who greeted the mistrial by 'shaking my head and saying "No, no, no", because it is such a monumental task arranging witnesses to testify from all over the United States – I just dreaded the thought of another trial.' Not surprisingly; for, as he also admits, 'the Menendez case played a big part in the destruction of my marriage. There were other problems, but my being absent – absent-minded as well as physically absent from family life –

caused my divorce. I lived the Menendez case for years, so my family life took a back seat.'

Jury selection for the second trial began in August 1995. One consequence of the high-profile defence team at the first trial was that the entire $14 million Menendez estate, already reduced by Lyle's penchant for buying Rolexes, Porsches and restaurants, had been swallowed up. For the second, the brothers' attorneys had to be paid by the taxpayers of Los Angeles, the court having found the defendants to be indigent.

Once more, jury selection moved slowly – but this time, Weissberg ruled there should be just the one, and that there should be a limit on the number of witnesses called on the subject of the alleged abuses. Possibly as a result (the total witness count dropped from 101 to 64) the second trial lasted a mere 23 weeks from 11 October 1995. The single jury began its deliberations on 1 March 1996 but on 14 March, two jurors had to be excused – one had had a heart attack, and another gone into premature labour. Two of the alternatives, who had, of course, heard all the evidence to allow for just such an eventuality, joined the panel, but the deliberations necessarily had to start all over again.

After just four days, they returned to the court. This time, the jurors had had little difficulty in finding both brothers guilty of two counts of first-degree murder and of conspiracy to commit murder. There are in California only two possible sentences that can be passed in cases of multiple murder for financial gain: life imprisonment without parole, or execution. But again, under California law, the same jury which reaches the verdict also re-assembles for what is known as the 'penalty phase.'

This time, the brothers got a little luckier. The jurors opted for life imprisonment. Afterwards, reports Les Zoeller, 'there was talk of the defence asking that the brothers be put together in one jail. The prosecution's thought and belief was that these two could not have a choice of anything in their life anywhere, and we were opposed to them being put in the same prison.'

The case had taken seven years out of Zoeller's life, and he deserves the last word on the Menendez brothers. 'Although I'm not a psychologist, I feel that Lyle is a true sociopath. I think that Erik was very weak, and was duped into committing the murders with Lyle. Lyle is just a cold-hearted murderer. It's just some chromosome missing in his soul.'

AILEEN WUORNOS –
THE TRUCKSTOP KILLER

During the Fall of 1990, the biggest serial murder investigation in America was centred on Gainesville, Florida. In the last week of August that year, the bodies of five college students – four girls and a boy – had turned up in three separate off-campus apartments. The girls had been sexually assaulted, stabbed and mutilated – indeed, one had been decapitated. There were no clues, no suspects, but an impressive posse of clamouring reporters from round the world.

These were young, attractive victims, killed in a spectacularly newsworthy way, and undoubtedly by the same murderer or murderers: the stuff of media frenzy.

Gainesville is in Marion County, and lies roughly halfway between the better-known centres of Orlando and Jacksonville. The Marion County Sheriff's Office was virtually under siege to report progress on the Gainesville slaughter, and quite understandably had no real wish to admit that, as it happened, they had another little problem brewing: one which would eventually put Gainesville in the shade, on the basis of the very same media-dominated criteria – only this time it would be the perpetrator, not the victims, who had the headline quality.

However, the local correspondent for Reuters, the international news agency, was under just as much pressure as the Gainesville cops to report some progress.

Michael Reynolds began combing through all the Florida local newspapers in search of anything else which might just tie in with the Gainesville case: homicides, missing persons, rapes – procedural work which the investigating officers were also no doubt doing, but certainly not then sharing with the media.

Reynolds spotted something very odd – not more student murders, but a quite different pattern of killings which also had a common theme. As he put it in his later book Dead Ends, 'bodies of white middle-age males with numerous bullets in them were being found throughout central Florida. Their abandoned vehicles were located miles from where they were killed. Some were nude; some were not. Two of the victims, and four of their vehicles, had been discovered in Marion County.' What he didn't spot at that time – and nor had the police – was that there had been an earlier case which conformed to exactly the same pattern, and which was to prove the linch-pin of the eventual conviction. But we'll come to that.

Reynolds contacted the Sheriff's spokesman, Sergeant Robert Douglas, and asked if the county had in fact got two entirely separate serial killers on its patch. Douglas did his best to dismiss the notion, and pointed out that the links between the various killings were so nebulous that there wasn't even a dedicated task force pursuing them as though they were indeed a single case.

Yet Reynolds was convinced that if he saw a connecting theme, surely the same thought must have leapt into the mind of any really experienced police officer. Small as some were, he had the cuttings from papers like the *Ocala Star-Banner*, and felt the pattern must surely be more than mere coincidence.

As far as he could see, the bodies of 43-year-old David Spears, found shot dead in Citrus County in June; of a male as yet unidentified, who would prove to be Charles Carskaddon, found shot dead in Pasco County in June; of Troy Burress, 50, found shot dead in Marion County in August; and of Dick Humphreys, 56, found shot dead in Marion County in September, raised at the very least an intriguing question or two. Throw in the fact that the car of a missing person, yet again a middle-aged man, once again travelling alone when last seen in June, had also turned up in Marion County in July, and it was well worth another phone call.

This time, Reynolds called the commander of the Marion County Sheriff's Criminal Investigation Division, Captain Steve Binegar. Now Binegar was already well aware that he and his colleagues in neighbouring counties almost certainly did have another serial killer on their hands, but until that moment they had all been agreed that the last thing their investigation needed was the intense media and political interest which was dogging the Gainesville inquiry.

On the other hand, they could none of them claim to have made great progress. Indeed, the detectives of Volusia County had spent months pursuing a suspect for their killing – the first, as it happened – who had nothing to do with it.

So, just as Binegar and his colleagues must have done when Reynolds approached them, let's review where things stood at that moment.

Detective Bob Kelley of Volusia County Sheriff's Office is proud to claim, 'I'm a fourth-generation police officer' and at the moment the body of Richard Mallory turned up concealed under some old carpet in thick woods north of Daytona Beach, could boast that he'd 'worked about 100 murders at that point.' Indeed, his long experience had already led him to expect the body to turn up somewhere, since Mallory's Cadillac had been found 12 days earlier in suspicious circumstances: 'backed into a wooded area; there were glasses that someone had attempted to bury, along with other personal items of Mallory – that alone leads you to believe that we're going to find a homicide', Kelley explains.

Oh – and there was blood behind the driver's seat.

Checks on Mallory had quickly turned up the facts that he ran a fairly erratic electronics repair-shop in Clearwater over to the West, and his virtually exclusive interest was in strip-clubs, pornography and prostitution. As Kelley recalls, 'It was at that point we started looking at the possibility that a female had killed him. And if he's from the Tampa Bay area, why was he in Daytona?' They also established that a camera and a radar detector, both of which Mallory habitually carried in his car, were missing.

Methodical checks around the topless clubs, plus a slip of paper found in Mallory's apartment, produced an apparent connection with a stripper implausibly named Chastity. Kelley and his colleagues soon developed strong suspicions that Chastity Lee Marcus might be the answer to their problem and spent several months trying to find enough evidence to win an indictment – which they did not, being eventually forced to recognize that although her lifestyle, like Mallory's, was far from blameless, she wasn't their murderer after all. Yet the feeling that it was a woman who had fired five .22 bullets into Mallory remained strong – not least because they had learned that he was known to be reluctant to have other men in his car, but ever-eager to get a woman in.

Still, their frequent contacts with colleagues across the state did pay off when one of them called from St Petersburg and asked Kelley: 'Are you aware that there are four other murders that are matching up very similar to what you're working, in the Marion County, Dixie County and Citrus County areas?'

At that point, Kelley says, 'I called over to the Marion County Sheriff's Office and started questioning them about their investigation and giving them information about ours, and found that they were identical. They had a lone male found in an isolated area, shot several times with a .22

calibre handgun; the ones that were fully dressed had their pockets pulled inside out; the car was found in a different location; they were men travelling by themselves; it just went on and on – they were pictures of Mallory's situation.'

After the disappointment of Chastity, remembers Kelley, 'It made us feel good that now we've got something to start working again; somewhere to go; another angle to start looking at. We met with the Marion County authorities, as well as Dixie County, Citrus County and Pasco County, and they had already started a task force, so we went over there to see what we could gain by getting involved.'

It has to be said that nobody had made all that much progress. Detective Jerry Thompson of Citrus County had taken the call late in the afternoon of 1 June 1990 which reported the discovery of a body, naked save for a baseball cap, in woodland 40 miles north of Tampa. In Florida's hot and humid climate, detectives have to develop strong stomachs. Bob Kelley had found his body in December, when, as he says, 'It's not tremendously cold, but it's cold enough to keep the body from decaying too much.' Jerry Thompson's summertime corpse was, he says 'in a mummified state. We weren't aware of the cause of death: we just didn't know, because of the decomposition of the body. Until the autopsy, we didn't know he was shot.'

What they did know was that 'we had some unusual things recovered at the crime scene – condoms, etcetera. And it kind of led us to believe that at least some female involvement was there.'

After the body was identified as Dave Spears, a construction worker from Orange County, Thompson established that when last seen he'd been driving a pick-up truck. And that had already turned up – abandoned on Interstate 75 in Marion County a week earlier, minus the set of tools which the practical Spears always had to hand: which, says the detective, 'told us that whoever was involved in the murder actually was with him in his vehicle at the time, and had left there after the murder and driven away in his truck.'

While checking on Spears' background and contacts in Sarasota, Thompson heard that Pasco County had just found a male body dumped off the Interstate, so on his way back he stopped by and met their investigating officer, Tom Muck. They went over the facts in the two cases and discovered a lot of similarities – not least, as Thompson notes, 'the projectiles were the same – so that's when we knew we had someone that was involved not just in our murder, but another murder also.'

Initially, Thompson had suspected the man who first discovered Spears' body, a surveyor called Matthew Cocking, in part because of his remarkably aggressive and foul-mouthed demeanour. But he abandoned that line rather more rapidly than Valusia County had given up on Chastity Marcus. The fact that Pasco County's body was another naked male lent support to the suspicion that a female was involved, although Tom Muck himself refused to rule out a homosexual crime of passion.

Citrus County were more open-minded. As Dayle Hinman, the state-wide co-ordinator of the crime analysis profile programme for the Florida Department of Law Enforcement, says: 'They will go out and seek assistance – they're very sharing-orientated, very professional.' They took their problem to Dayle, who had been trained by the FBI, shortly after the Spears killing.

'What profiling is essentially based on', she explains 'is being a historian and looking at the cases. The FBI came up with the idea that if a crime occurs in a certain way to a certain type of victim and the same type of injuries are received, and the same individual would do it, then if you can keep statistics on this and you can do studies on the kind of people, then you can theorize that the next time this type of crime occurs it will be the same kind of person for the same kind of reason.'

She applied that basic insight to the facts Citrus County made available. They had, she says 'done a wonderful job with their crime-scene pictures' and she concluded 'because of the way the victim was lying and that he was nude and had his baseball cap on still, what we thought had taken place was that he had taken the clothes off himself and then put the baseball cap back on, and the perpetrator would be a female. I can't think of any other reason for him to be in that location at that time without his clothes, and with his hat on.'

What's more, contrary to Tom Muck's suspicions, Hinman trusted Citrus County's background research which had revealed 'no indication that Mr Spears was a homosexual, so there was no reason for him to go into that wooded area with another man.'

Having concluded that the killer was, on balance, likely to be female, Hinman went on to consider the historical record of women killers. 'Historically, most of the women who have killed multiple times would be the kind of individual who would be, say, a nurse in a nursing home who decides that people are in pain, so overdoses them in medication, or a woman who kills multiple husbands, for insurance, or a day-care worker who is responsible for the smothering death of multiple children – when most cases are ruled to be sudden infant death syndrome, or SIDS. This was the first person we'd ever become involved with who was a predatory serial killer, so that's unusual.'

Hinman's encyclopaedic, and inevitably rather dispassionate, knowledge of the art of murder led her to other conclusions. She certainly took the view that 'the ability to lure the victim into a wooded area and have them disrobed would be more of a woman type of crime', but she went further. A convinced believer in sharing information – something that not all detectives from county-wide jurisdictions endorsed – she took a broad-brush view of the facts available and decided: 'The perpetrator of these crimes was a murderer who robbed; not a person who was taking these men with their vehicles to get their personal belongings, their effects, their money. They weren't robberies where people just ended up getting killed – it was a murderer who robbed. All the people that were associated with the task force saw the perpetrator to be a predator, because if she wanted just money then she could have waited till people parked their cars at rest stops and broken in. She could have broken into homes: she could have done a robbery with a gun and then left with the money.'

One other bonus that Hinman's profiling offered those agencies which would listen was this: 'If everyone can agree that the perpetrator is male or female, you cut the population of suspects in half.'

Nevertheless, as if there weren't enough different Florida jurisdictions and investigating agencies involved, it was to emerge later that on 5 May, the Georgia Bureau of Investigation had opened its file on an unidentified white male corpse found shot in the woods just off Interstate 75 – in Brooks County, right across the state line from Florida. When the information came through in a routine circular seeking leads, Muck called them, and established that Georgia's nameless victim had also been nude, and shot by a .22.

Even for those detectives who did by now recognize that they were tackling a very mobile serial killer, life wasn't getting any easier. Marion County, for example, had acquired another case on 5 April, when the body of a man called Giddens was found in his car: shot, but only once, through the head, not the body, and with a .38, not a .22. And not only had his car not been taken, but it hadn't been stripped of either its identification tags, or indeed, $1,000 in bills in the glove compartment. After a while, it was agreed that it was probably an entirely separate case, very possibly linked to drug-dealing, but even reaching that conclusion had occupied valuable time for the task force team.

In fact, the first real break in the case came not with a murder, but with a traffic accident. On 4 July 1990, America's Independence Day holiday, the Bailey family was enjoying the break at their home near Orange Springs in the Ocala National Forest when they heard a screech of tyres from the bend on the road outside. Rhonda Bailey wasn't surprised – that particular curve had seen many accidents – but she and her husband naturally went out to see what had happened, and if their help was needed.

There, they saw not just a car skidding off the road and into the brush, but two women emerging from it, throwing beer cans into the undergrowth and cursing each other. One, blonde, was bleeding from a wound to her arm: the other, with reddish-brown hair, seemed unhurt. The blonde asked Bailey not to call the police, and claimed to have family staying nearby. Then the two got back into the car, despite its broken windscreen and dented bodywork, and somehow managed to back it out on to the road again.

It didn't get very far before expiring. The women abandoned it beside the road a little further on, and when a local fireman who'd been called about the accident saw two women pedestrians as he drove towards the site of the reported smash, and stopped to ask if they had been involved, they denied it, and told him with some vehemence that they certainly didn't need any help.

The car was a 1988 Pontiac Sunbird, and its licence plate was missing. Using the chassis number, Marion County were able to trace it to a Peter Siems, a 65-year old retired merchant seaman from Jupiter, Florida, who spent much of his time working as a missionary. What's more, Mr Siems, who had left home on 7 June to visit relatives in Arkansas, had never reached them, and had been reported missing on 22 June.

That was more than enough to set bells ringing in the various sheriff's offices. Jerry Thompson in Citrus County heard from Marion County about the wreck and joined his colleagues there to give it a thorough examination. On the underside of the door handle, they turned up a bloody fingerprint which, as he says 'was very crucial.'

But even better – since, of course, nobody at that stage had a suspect whose prints could be compared – was that between the Baileys and local fire chief Hubert Hewitt, Marion County officers had fairly detailed descriptions of the two women, and had had composite pictures of the identikit type made.

Jupiter is in Palm Beach County, more than 200 miles south of Orange Springs, so this development brought in yet another force. While the Marion and Citrus and Pasco detectives argued the merits of issuing the composites to the press and public, Detective John Wisnieski of Jupiter put out a nationwide teletype message to all of America's 17,000-odd law enforcement agencies, with descriptions of the two women (who, he said, 'appeared to be lesbians'), and completed a 17-page Violent Criminal Apprehension Program Analysis Report which he sent off to the Florida Department of Law Enforcement.

Clues might still be a little thin on the ground, but investigating agencies were beginning to back up round the block.

As were victims. Marion County found another one on 4 August. By now, they weren't surprised. Delivery driver Troy Burress had been reported missing in the early morning of 31 July, and his abandoned vehicle had been discovered a few hours later some 20 miles east of Ocala. The body itself was discovered in the Ocala National Forest, some eight miles away from the truck. Again, the Florida climate had made identification difficult, but Mrs Burress had no doubts that it was her husband's wedding ring the police recovered. Rather more surprising in the circumstances – lone male, abandoned vehicle, and death caused by shooting with a .22 pistol – the investigator, John Tilley, at first suspected a hitchhiker called Curtis Michael Blankenship.

It didn't take long for Blankenship to join Chastity and Cocking in the Abandoned file: nor, unfortunately, for another victim to turn up. The body of Dick Humphreys, a 56-year old former policeman now working as a protective investigator for the Florida Department of Health, was found in Marion County on 12 September. He'd been shot seven times with a .22, and his car didn't turn up for another week, this time in Suwanee County.

The Humphreys case was the last to catch the inquisitive eye of Michael Reynolds before he made his initial approach to Captain Binegar, whom he interviewed by telephone on 6 November. The next day, despite Binegar's very cautious responses, Reuters carried a brief story which revealed for the first time that 'an eight-month string of unsolved murders has left investigators in north-central Florida facing the possibility of a serial killer – or killers – preying upon highway travellers throughout the region', but did not mention the possibility that the killer was female.

Then, on 19 November, the body of Walter Gino Antonio, naked save for a pair of socks, was found in remote woods in Dixie County by a Tampa police officer who was spending his day off hunting. Antonio, 60, was a trucker, and a member of the Reserve Police. He'd been shot four times – with a .22.

His car turned up five days later, abandoned more than 200 miles away in Brevard County. Two days later, Reynolds finally managed to reach Binegar on the phone and ask for a full face-to-face interview. Binegar agreed, and set the date for the following evening. It rather seems that the Marion County Captain did not, however, share this fact with all his colleagues from the ever-expanding task force.

Equally, when Reynolds arrived and the two men talked through all the available facts and theories, Steve Binegar took his own unilateral decision on what he should share with the reporter and what he should allow to be made public. Most important of all, he gave Reynolds the two composites of the women sighted at the crashing of Peter Siems' car, and full descriptions. And then, as Reynolds reported, he asked: 'Do you think we can get some press coverage around the state on this ?'

Reynolds' response was immediate. 'Serial killings with two female suspects? You'll have all that you want – more than you want.' Binegar suddenly saw the spectre of the Gainesville feeding frenzy, and asked how that could be avoided. Again, the experienced Reynolds responded. 'Get out front on it. Be prepared. Call a press conference.'

There were three immediate consequences. Reuters put out the story, and the composites; some members of the task force, particularly Jerry Thompson and Tom Muck, blew their tops with Binegar for going public; and in the following three weeks, more than 400 leads were phoned in to the Sheriff's Office.

The two women were obviously fairly memorable characters. A trailer-rental firm in Homosassa Springs thought the composites looked remarkably like two customers they'd had the previous year. The names they had given were Tyria Moore and Lee. A motel owner south of Ocala offered the information that the composites strongly suggested two casual workers she'd employed – called Tyria Moore and Susan Blahovec. An anonymous caller offered the names of Ty Moore and Lee Blahovec. They were lesbians, she said, but Lee Blahovec worked tricks as a prostitute at truckers' cafes.

Even better, the police in Port Orange, near Daytona, reported that they had actually been watching a suspicious couple, called Lee Blahovec and Tyria Moore, and could let the investigators have a note of their movements in recent months. They had mostly stayed at the Fairview Motel in Harbor Oaks, where Blahovec had registered as Cammie Marsh Greene.

It didn't take long for computer checks with the driving licence records, and criminal records, to establish that while neither had any serious previous record in Florida – though

Moore had once had burglary charges against her dropped – the photographs on the licences of Blahovec and Greene did not tally.

Bob Kelley remembers how good it felt to finally have a solid lead. 'We had been working a murder for over a year, we wanted to do whatever we could to try to solve it and we were getting different people saying that the suspects were in the Harbor Oaks area of Daytona, so the decision was made to move the entire task force over to Daytona Beach.'

Which is, of course, in Kelley's own patch of Volusia County. And, armed now with both the driving-licence photographs and some names, his force began to check around the pawn shops, just in case the women had converted some of the missing items into quick cash.

In fairly short order, they turned up Richard Mallory's camera and radar-detector and David Spears' tool-kit. The person pledging the items had called herself Cammie Marsh Greene. And, thanks to the Florida regulations for pawn-shops, Cammie Marsh Greene had been obliged to put her thumb-print on the receipt she'd given the broker.

It was by now very close to Christmas, and Jenny Ahern of the crime laboratory at the Florida Department of Law Enforcement recalls how she was looking forward to the break when the call came in late on Friday, 21 December. 'The Sheriff's Office asked us to run the print on that pawn-shop ticket through our automated finger-print system, which we call AFIS, which has a database of prints of people who have prior criminal histories in the state of Florida. We

diligently searched that print for several hours through the
system, and were not successful in identifying her. So, very
off the cuff and thinking, "Oh, this'll never happen", I said to
the investigators that after Christmas we could go to the
different county agencies where you know she's been, and if
they have a master-file we could do a search. A master-file is
for when you know the classification of a fingerprint: you can
search all the prints that might have that classification –
which would be an enormous task, because all we had was
one finger and it's a whorl; that's all we knew, so you're
having to look at at least 50 per cent of all the files in every
agency we'd have to go to. I never thought when I said it that
what the detective would say was, "Good: we'll see you
tomorrow at the Volusia County Sheriff's Department." '

'I said, "But Christmas is only four days away; Santa Claus
is coming", but they pointed out the seriousness of this, so I
assigned two colleagues to go with me, and the next morning
we went to Volusia County to look for her. My partners were
a little bit reluctant, as I was, because we were looking for
the proverbial needle in the haystack, and we didn't even
know if the needle was in the haystack.'

Jenny and her team knew there were tens of thousands of
fingerprint cards to go through, and weren't cheered to discover
that Volusia hadn't even separated the males and females.
Nevertheless they each took a batch and started work. Ahern
herself took her first batch – 'a hundred to a hundred and fifty
cards ' – and started flipping through them.

'I was in the files for 15 minutes and, all of a sudden, there she was! I couldn't breathe: it was like, "This just cannot be happening that quick." And I turned the card over, and sure enough it was a white female. Well, at that point in time I screamed, "Yes! Santa Claus is coming this year!"'

Jenny rang the task force and told them she needed to see them – but said, 'I don't think we'd better tell you why on the phone: just meet us right away.'

The name on the card wasn't Blahovec or Greene, but Lori Grody, who'd been arrested in 1986 while driving a stolen car and carrying a loaded .22 revolver. But the photograph of Grody taken at the time matched that on the Blahovec driver's licence. What's more, there was still an outstanding warrant for Grody, who had violated probation.

Grody's prints were sent back to the lab to see if any matches could be found with the various prints lifted from the victims' cars. They could – the bloody print in Peter Siems' wrecked Sunbird was Grody's. Furthermore, now armed with prints and a choice of aliases, it was worth asking the National Crime Information Centre to circulate the entire country. Blahovec/Greene/Grody was, they soon heard, actually Aileen Carol Wuornos, born on 29 February in the leap year of 1956, in Rochester, Michigan. She'd begun acquiring a record while still at school – truancy, shoplifting and burglary.

Her adult record was, however, rather more serious. From Colorado to Michigan to Florida, she'd left a trail of arrests, jumped bail and used yet more false names. And of the 14 incidents the search had turned up, six involved firearms.

There still remained a problem for the detectives: finding Wuornos, and finding the gun. As soon as the Christmas and New Year holidays were over, they concentrated their forces on the streets of Port Orange. In addition to regular uniformed and plain-clothes surveillance, the decision had been taken to put in undercover officers who could blend in with the offbeat clientèle of the bars which, mounting evidence suggested, would appeal to Wuornos both socially and professionally.

One of them is usually referred to as Mike Joyner but, understandably, he prefers not to give anyone his real name. Now a Lieutenant with a narcotics task force, he's been working under cover for around 25 years: as he says, 'I try to live the life or get in the minds of people that commit crimes. I dress different; I look different. Our primary duty in special investigations is doing undercover operations, whether it'd be contract killings or serial killers, regular homicides, narcotics.'

In this case, the hunch was that the sleazier the bar, the better the chance of spotting Wuornos, so Joyner and his colleague Dick Martin, bearded and unkempt, decided that they'd best present themselves in the rougher spots of Ridgwood Avenue, where a sighting of Wuornos had been phoned in, as just a couple of visiting drug-dealers down from Georgia and looking for a good time. Just to help, they went by the names of Bucket and Drums.

They were, of course, provided with extensive back-up. As Joyner says, 'If any undercover officer ever tells you they're not scared, he just told you a fat-ass lie.' But the capacity for multi-agency operations like this to screw up cannot be over-estimated. For all the officers to keep in touch, they needed mobile phones. Those were supplied by the Florida Department of Law Enforcement – and, as Thompson recalls, the FDLE, based in Tampa, had produced a bunch of phones which were all on the 813 Tampa area code, 'so we've got to dial up long-distance every time we make a call!'

Bucket and Drums cruised the area for a while, getting no joy at the bar where Wuornos had allegedly been spotted; and then, on the evening of 8 January, sighted a blonde in the doorway of the Port Orange Pub and took a chance. They went in, and asked the barkeeper who the blonde was. 'That's Lee', he said. Even better, she'd obviously been drinking for a while, and it wasn't difficult for Joyner to persuade her not just to take drink from him (deliberately flashing his large bankroll) but to dance with him to the lachrymose country hits he played on the jukebox. On her forehead was the distinctive scar that the witnesses to her car crash had noted. The undercover cops seized a moment to make a long-distance call to their colleagues just around the corner and pass on the news that they hadn't just found the suspect, they were partying with her.

Things were looking good, but then they suddenly were not. To Joyner's horror, some uniformed police from the local Port Orange force, who had not actually been informed of the extensive undercover operation, came into the bar, following up a tip-off, and hustled Wuornos out into their squad-car. Martin managed to get Jerry Thompson on his mobile and explain, in quite heated language, what was happening. At this stage, the last thing anyone needed was for Wuornos to be arrested when the investigators didn't have Moore, didn't have the gun and very possibly couldn't even get an indictment.

Thompson couldn't quite think what to do, save be pleased that, for once, complete operational secrecy had actually been maintained. So he rang Kelley, who miraculously remembered the Port Orange PD's number. He called them and, after pulling heavy rank, managed to get the dispatcher there to call off her officers. Wuornos came back into the pub and told Bucket and Drums it had all been a mistake. In fact, she said, 'You know what? They thought I was that serial killer going around shooting all those guys.'

Wuornos had introduced herself to the 'Georgia drug-dealers' as Lee Blahovec, but she'd identified herself to the Port Orange cops as Cammie Marsh Greene. After a few more beers at Joyner's expense, she announced she had to go. The officers offered her a lift, but she declined, and set off, clutching a small suitcase.

Joyner and Martin naturally followed – and, to their renewed horror, they saw an unmarked car with two FDLE officers inside proceed to track her with its lights turned off. Once again, the cellular phones began to run red-hot all over the State until the FDLE car was ordered to withdraw and its occupants to leave the investigation they had endangered.

The operation wasn't just at risk from the multiplicity of agencies involved – or feeling they should be involved. Getting pally with Aileen Wuornos, even aided by a taxpayers' bankroll, was proving pretty demanding. At the end of it all, Mike Joyner explained, 'we spent three days and nights in the bar. I would buy beer, cigarettes, whatever she wanted; we shot pool a lot; we constantly played the jukebox. We drank all the time – I mean, I've been around a long time and I've seen a lot of things, but I ain't ever seen one woman drink more beer than that woman – I thought I was pretty stout at it, but I couldn't hold a bucket of water to a cup of piss to her. The final day, we were in the bar drinking, and I was feeling when I got through this detail, somebody was going to have to put me in detox, because I had drunk more than I had in the last year.'

But despite the alcoholic haze which surrounded him, Joyner very clearly recalled that 'Aileen had told me a key she had hanging on her belt-loop held the story of her life.' He was very eager to see what lock that key might unlock.

Then, on that third day, by now in a biker bar called The Last Resort, the situation took another dramatic turn. Despite the task force theory that this fish was best played long and slow, Joyner discovered that that evening as many as 150 bikers were expected to turn up for a giant barbecue. 'My concern', he says, 'is that if Aileen all of a sudden sees another man with more money than I had, she would go to him, and there's no way I could get her back. And if she got on the back of a bike and put her helmet on and rode off at midnight, there's just no way the team would ever know. So at that point I said to her I was tired and needed to get something to eat, and why didn't I get her a motel room, because she needed to take a bath and change clothes? So I left and and got a motel room and came back and gave her the key. And the decision was taken to arrest her when she left.'

With professional pride, Joyner now says: 'I don't think she ever suspected me of being a law enforcement officer – I really don't.' And to keep his cover, when the surveillance team closed in on Wuornos they arrested them both, and threw them both into the back seat of the squad car. Joyner knew his curiosity about that key was about to be satisfied.

Still, no gun, and not enough real evidence: but the hunt for Moore had made progress. Shortly after Wuornos was arrested on that old outstanding warrant, Jerry Thompson flew to Pennsylvania. Moore was apparently living with her sister in Scranton. Having first arranged with the local police to pick her up and take her to a motel, Thompson and a colleague drove there, introduced themselves and read Moore her rights, although they did not actually charge her. They needed help and co-operation – rather than another under-evidenced case – which they very quickly got.

Moore began talking in the Scranton motel, kept on talking on the flight back to Florida and talked still more once safely housed in Daytona. She had also helped by giving the detectives a burgundy-coloured briefcase which Wuornos had given her. They recognized it as the one Dick Humphreys was carrying when last seen alive.

Meantime, an undercover woman officer who'd been sharing Wuornos' cell reported she'd not managed to get anything incriminating out of her. Thompson put it to Moore that she should phone Wuornos in jail, and see if she could do better. 'I was quite confident she would help', he says. 'Tyria Moore was a personable person: you could tell she wasn't directly involved with the murders. She was OK.'

The line Moore should take had been agreed by the team, and she had been coached in it. She was to tell Wuornos that she was frightened the murders would be pinned on her, and hope that this would persuade Wuornos to confess to take Moore off that hook.

The first call didn't make much progress, since Wuornos still thought she was only being held on that old Lori Grody warrant. But the calls went on for three days, with Moore ever more insistent that she feared she would be arrested, and did not want to go to jail for crimes she had not committed. Slowly, Wuornos came to realize what was expected of her; and eventually the secret audience listening in heard her say to Ty, 'Just go ahead and let them know what they want to know and I'll cover for you, because you're innocent. I'm not going to let you go to jail. Listen: if I have to confess, I will.'

She was as good as her word. From 16 January on, she began talking to the police with such abandon that her attorney from the public defender's office tried in vain to make her shut up. But she insisted on stressing, over and over again, not only that Moore had had nothing to do with any of it (although, of course, with her guilty knowledge she could still have faced charges as an accessory), but that she, Wuornos, had in every single case killed in self-defence. Her story was that all the men, clothed or naked, had either threatened her, assaulted her or raped her.

At long last the case was falling into place. During her phone conversations with Moore, Wuornos had let drop the fact that she had 'given that water-pistol away' and encouraged Moore to break into her storage locker to help herself to items she wanted. Too late: the key which had fascinated Joyner had already been recognized as one for such a storage locker, a search warrant had been obtained and the FDLE were now in possession of all manner of items, from Richard Mallory's razor to Walter Antonio's police baton. In fact, the inventory ran to seven pages. As she had said, that key held the story of her life.

The news that the task force had finally got their woman – that, indeed, the killings had been carried out by a lone woman – came as a huge relief to the people of Florida: so much so that in a number of the papers there, Aileen Wuornos, 'Truck Stop Killer', prostitute and lesbian, took front-page precedence over the opening of the Gulf War, which delighted her. Indeed, her appetite for sensational self-publicity was so great that she made the sensational claim to have slept with more than 250,000 men, which not every paper bothered to work out was impossible – it would have required 35 clients a day, every day, for 20 years.

Since the evidence looked strongest in the case of Richard Mallory, the decision was taken to try that case, and rely on the confessions in the others to elicit guilty pleas from Wuornos. Most of the counties involved were actually prepared to trade a complete set of guilty pleas for life imprisonment, but one prosecuting attorney refused to strike the deal, insisting that she face the death penalty.

So, almost a year to the day since she began confessing, Aileen Wuornos went on trial for the murder of Richard Mallory. By now, the .22 had been recovered from the waters of Rose Bay near Harbor Oaks, along with various other items which were traced back to victims, and Wuornos had another problem, in the form of Florida's 'Williams Rule'. That states that evidence of other crimes than the one on the indictment may be introduced if it helps to substantiate a pattern.

Without it, it's just possible her claim to have slain Mallory in self-defence might have impressed a jury. Mallory's own character was not, after all, pristine: indeed, it was later to emerge that he had once received ten years in jail for sexual assault, but that didn't come in time to help the defendant. After less than a fortnight's trial, the jury took just two hours to find her guilty of first-degree murder – at which point, oblivious of the fact that they had still to consider the penalty, she screamed from the dock: 'I'm innocent! I was raped! I hope you get raped! Scumbags of America!'

The next day, the jurors unanimously voted for the death sentence. Over the next ten months she faced no new trials, pleading either 'no contest' or 'guilty' to the murders of Humphreys, Burress, Spears, Carskaddon and Antonio, and was handed five more sentences of death.

In the circumstances, there was little point in charging her for the murder of Peter Siems, whose body had never been found, although nobody in the case had the slightest doubt that he, too, had picked up the wrong hitchhiker, and been shot somewhere in the endless woods of Florida or neighbouring Georgia.

Sentenced to death on six counts, Wuornos and her lawyers fought the customary rearguard action through the courts for the next ten years, until she herself gave up the struggle, dismissed her attorneys, waived her remaining rights of appeal – and was adjudged sane after one final stay of execution for psychiatric examination. On 9 October 2002, she was executed by lethal injection. Despite her confessions, and ultimate acquiescence, there had been a world-wide campaign to justify her acts, and save her life, on the grounds of her alleged 'victim status'. And after her death, there were those who claimed her execution had been a cynical exercise to attract votes for the State Governor, facing re-election the following month.

He, by the way, was Jeb Bush, better known perhaps for his brother, George W. Bush, and the mystery of the 'hanging chads' in Florida's polling booths.

IVAN MILAT –
THE BACKPACKER MURDERER

The Belanglo State Forest, a couple of hours south of Sydney in New South Wales, covers some 40,000 acres; ideal for wildlife, for naturalists and for orienteering, the sport which demands both stamina and sharp navigational skills.

And that's why, on Saturday, 19 September 1992, experienced orienteer Ken Seily was, for once, not running his challenging course alone, but was accompanied by a novice, Keith Caldwell, eager to learn the ropes. In Australia, of course, September is glorious Springtime, not Autumn, and Ken Seily remembers that the forest was looking magnificently lush. By the afternoon, the two men had reached a striking landmark called Executioner's Drop and were taking their bearings on the next designated check-point, marked by a large boulder, when Ken smelled the unmistakable rotting odour of decomposition.

Familiar with the forest as he was, and its large population of kangaroos, wallabies and dingos, Ken assumed that somewhere in the bush around him an animal had died. The relatively inexperienced Keith Caldwell found the stench more striking and, in particular, that it grew worse as they rounded the boulder.

Slowing down, they suddenly saw a pile of forest litter, heaped up as though deliberately. It was some seven feet long and two feet high, and sticking out of it there seemed to be a bone and some hair. Which still didn't rule out an animal – but their next sightings in the mound certainly did. Kangaroos don't wear T-shirts, nor shoes.

In the wilderness of the forest, a chance discovery was itself improbable. That it should be made by two men equipped with compasses and a detailed map was almost miraculous. Having carefully plotted the location, Ken and Keith hurried off to rendezvous with the other members of the orienteering club at the final check-point. As soon as they told what they had seen, and suspected, everyone agreed that the authorities should be informed as quickly as possible. Using a mobile phone, Ken rang the emergency services, whose operator immediately asked, 'Is this an emergency?'

In the circumstances, Ken's possibly over-rational answer, 'Not really', was true enough – but to his amazement, the operator promptly rang off. It took him several more attempts before he finally got through to the police station in Bowral, and this time had the wit to begin by announcing 'I've found a body in the Belanglo Forest.'

Uniformed police quickly drove out to the forest's edge where Seily was waiting, and using torchlight in the advancing evening gloom, were led to the site, marking their trail with reflective tape. Gradually, they were joined first by detectives from Bowral, then a scene-of-crime unit from Goulburn and finally by men from the regional homicide squad, who put in calls both to the Sydney police and to the Missing Persons Bureau.

One of the detectives from Goulburn was Andrew Grosse, who can still recall the phone call which came in that evening as he was just sitting down to dinner. 'I had to respond, and I was taken to an area that I'd never heard of before, that I didn't know existed. I'd obviously been told there was a body in the forest, and you immediately start thinking when you hear those things, "Well, we've got a murder here; we've got an unnatural death." And that's the pinnacle of my work – investigating murder crime scenes.'

If Grosse, and presumably many of his colleagues, was ignorant of the hidden world within the forest they, the media and the Australian public were going to become steadily more familiar with it over the next two years. As more and more bodies came to light, what became known as The Backpacker Murders evoked horror round the world – not least because the victims included young people from Germany and Britain, as well as Australia itself.

Curiously, Australia has quite a record for mass murder. There's even a specifically Australian term for it, which I've not seen used by British or American police – 'multicide'. And the first recorded case took place in Tasmania in 1822, barely a generation after the first European settlers, voluntary or compulsory, began to arrive.

Just one body doesn't suggest a multicide, of course. Grosse began his work with no inkling of what lay in store. 'When I arrived at the scene, nothing had been set up to keep people out, so that was one of the first things I did. The next thing I had to do was define a point of entry – that's the site or path that people use to get into the scene, and part of the process is searching along that path, making sure that the way we're going to be using is not destroying any physical evidence. When I arrived, it was quite difficult to see what we had using torchlight. We could see that we had a pile of sticks and branches underneath a rock ledge, and obviously it was unnatural: it couldn't have happened unless someone had done it. When we got closer in, we could see an elbow and the back of a head, but at that stage we didn't know whether it was a male or female. Obviously we took off the layers of sticks carefully, just making sure that there was nothing that was being lost, and then we were confronted with an almost intact, preserved body of a female, lying on her stomach, still fully clothed. And I remember thinking, "How long has this person been here?" and I estimated within two or three weeks, based on the decomposition, but we later found out she'd been there five months, which was a bit surprising.'

It had, of course, been through the months of the Australian winter, which was to help Peter Bradhurst, the forensic pathologist to whom the body was taken by the government undertaker after the police had carefully extricated it from the heap of forest litter. 'Even though she was in a state of decomposition, there was one aspect that was helpful', he explains. 'There was partial mummification, and this had preserved the shape of the stab wounds we found, and so we were able to measure these, and were able to see whether a double-edged or single-edged blade had been used. We could see that a single-edged knife had been used.'

To terrible effect. She had received multiple wounds, most of them to her back. As Bradhurst points out, 'The stab wounds to the spine would have paralysed her, and made her unable to move.' There were other wounds, both on her sides and on her front. As Bradhurst was about to phone the police with his initial report that Sunday morning, however, they called him. A second body had been found.

Andrew Grosse had closed down the floodlit crime scene on Saturday night after the first body had been removed, and the following morning at around nine o'clock, two members of the searching party combing the undergrowth in daylight for any further evidence, stumbled across a large log, and a similar pile of bracken, only 100 feet away from the first. Sticking out was a leg, again with its shoe still on.

Missing persons records had already turned up the fact that two British backpackers, Caroline Clarke and Joanne Walters, both aged 22, had not been seen since they left Sydney five months earlier, telling friends they intended to hitch-hike to Melbourne to look for work. They weren't the only missing backpackers on file, but by Sunday afternoon positive identification had been made, and no one as yet was wondering quite what might have happened to the others.

This time, Bradhurst travelled down to Belanglo himself, examined both grave sites and supervised the removal of the second body. He quickly discovered from x-rays that while the first victim (who was soon to be identified as Joanne Walters) had been viciously stabbed to death: the second, Caroline Clarke, had been shot. There was one stab wound on her body, but she had been shot ten times in the head. As Grosse says, 'I remember thinking, "Well, one shot would have killed her – why nine more?"'

When the news of the first body's discovery broke, Detective Gerrard Dutton of the Forensic Ballistics Unit in Sydney was driving on his way to a job in the nearby Blue Mountains, idly listening to the news on the car radio. 'When the report came on that they'd found this decomposing body in a forest, I joked to my colleague that I hoped that the victim hadn't been shot, because what that would mean is that we'd be required to attend the morgue in the next day or so for a fairly foul-smelling autopsy.'

As, indeed, he was; though not, of course, for that first gruesome discovery, Joanne Walters, but for that of Caroline. He, too, was struck by the sheer number of bullets fired. 'We found seven bullets at the autopsy, but it showed us that she'd been shot ten times from three different angles – from the left, the right, and the rear – and these shots were grouped together. The interesting aspect was that when we found the spent cases at the crime scene, they were only a few metres away from the body, and they were all grouped in a small area, which meant that the killer had to have been standing more or less in the one spot for them to be ejected in that position. That meant that the body must have been moved in between the shots occurring.'

The only conclusion from that had to be that the murderer (or murderers – after all, there were two distinct methods of execution) had cold-bloodedly used the corpse of Caroline Clarke for – well, target practice.

Out at the scene, Dutton found three bullets in the soil underneath where Caroline's head had lain, so now he had all ten. But he also used his metal-detector to find as many spent casings as he could, and recalls that 'even looking at them at the scene, I was very familiar with that type of firing-pin impression, because it's a unique shape that is only used in a Ruger Model 10-22 rifle. Later in the laboratory, when I examined these features more closely, I was happy that the 10-22 Ruger was by far the most likely firearm responsible.'

So called because it has a ten-shot magazine and fires a .22-calibre round, that model of rifle from the American firm of Ruger is, and has been, very popular. His confidence that he had identified it may have given Dutton professional satisfaction, but it was to give many of his colleagues hours of fruitless work contacting arms dealers and gun clubs: more than 40,000 of the weapons had been imported into Australia.

While police combed the crime scene for further evidence – or bodies – they also sought advice elsewhere. Forensic psychiatrist Dr Rod Milton was asked to visit the scene and draw his own conclusions. He not only talked to Andrew Grosse, who gave him a gruesome guided tour of the sealed-off area of forest, but saw Grosse's drawings, of which he says: 'Admittedly, a drawing means an interpretation, but an accurate drawing is usually worth a lot more than a photograph because it gives depth and understanding.'

Milton explains that his approach is one of formulating a picture, but one which is 'a bit like a garment that has gaps in it – if you like, glimpses – and one glimpse I had after talking with Andy Grosse about Caroline's body, and how the cartridges were all found in one spot, and how the bullets were fired, was of deliberate cold action, with considerable enjoyment on the part of the person who did it. The other thing was, why would someone continue to fire shots into the cranium of a dead person? So it suggests an absorption with weapons – weapons for their own sake.'

The psychiatrist also began to entertain a notion that still hangs in the air to this day. 'It's very hard to imagine one person carrying out two totally different sets of behaviours (the ferocious stabbing of one victim and the clinical shooting of the other): not impossible, but a bit hard to swallow.'

In fact, Milton told the police that he thought the best explanation, or the most economical explanation of the data, 'was that two people were involved. That allowed for the deliberate, cold kind of person who seeks power on the one hand, and the explosive, aggressive person on the other.'

While the psychiatrist was musing on the conflicting

signals the crimes sent out, all around him police were methodically searching the forest. Forty officers were assigned to sift a strip 500 feet wide and one and a half miles long. Very close to the makeshift grave of Caroline Clarke, six cigarette stubs were found, all of the same brand, which certainly suggested the killer or killers had been in no hurry. Even more bizarre, around 40 yards from the scene, someone had built a fireplace from loose house-bricks.

The search took almost a week, but did not turn up any more of the two victims' property or camping gear. Nor, to the detectives' relief, any more bodies. In fact, they allowed the media to understand that they no longer feared any more bodies were likely to be found.

Grosse remembers rather graphically just how things then developed. 'At the time when the bodies were found, it was quite frenetic. Obviously a lot of work was being done at the sites, during the post mortems, and assessing the information that was coming in from the public. Things had to be followed up; investigations had to be carried out on sightings. So a small task force of investigators were given the task of following up leads, putting out public appeals, looking at all the records, going over what had been done, just to see whether anything had been missed. The investigation carried on, and after a while, it struck a hiatus; it started to die down, information stopped coming in. The investigations that people were looking into were either dispelled or put on the back burner because no more could be done. I suppose after about nine or ten months, it was all put on the back burner. It was never forgotten, but it was put on the back burner.'

The heat was dramatically raised in October 1993 – a little over a year since those first discoveries, and a month or two after the investigation had run out of steam. Bruce Pryor habitually scavenged his firewood from the Belanglo Forest, and knew it as well as most – but there were still places he had never been. That October Tuesday, he took a track off one of the major fire trails he'd never previously tried. It quickly opened on to a rocky clearing, and he noticed with surprise that somebody had built a fireplace there, using scattered rocks.

He stopped his truck, and looked around. As he circled the clearing, he suddenly saw a large bone on the ground. It didn't look to him like one from a kangaroo – in fact, it looked suspiciously like a human thigh-bone. He continued wandering, taking a slightly different route back to his vehicle – and then what he saw was unmistakable – it was a human skull. Not quite as confident as the orienteers had been, he didn't mark the spot, but decided instead to take the skull with him as he drove out of the forest to make his report.

His first call was to Bowral detectives, but there was no answer. So he rang the police station, and told them that he had found parts of a skeleton.

Soon after, a squad car turned up with two uniformed constables, who seemed a little sceptical. When Pryor produced his skull, however, they quickly raised the detectives on their radio. When they arrived, they asked Pryor to take them back to the site. As Pryor showed Detective Peter

Lovell where he'd found the skull and the long bone, Detective Steven Murphy walked round the clearing and into the edges of the surrounding bush. After a while, he came back to report what he'd seen: a pile of brush, with a pair of sandshoes sticking out.

The New South Wales Police rapidly realized that they had been mistaken in two important ways: one, they'd down-played the earlier discoveries; and two, they'd invited a much more rigorous media vigilation of what they now did.

An investigation which had quietly wound down now became a major priority. And that was only the beginning. Two more bodies, bad enough: five, a crisis. It might even be suggested by the uncharitable, a panic. For each new body that was found, it seems a new escalation of the number of detectives involved ensued. And sleepy Bowral, which for the preceding 60 years had only ever been mentioned in the world's press as the birthplace of the great batsman Don Bradman, had to adjust to an influx of crime reporters rather than cricket pilgrims.

When the first two bodies, Walters and Clarke, were found, early inquiries to the Missing Persons Bureau had certainly revealed that they weren't the only backpackers to have disappeared, but as they were speedily identified from dental records the investigation had focussed very much on them, and not much time had been spent wondering about the others. Now that had changed, since there appeared to be several possible candidates for the latest finding.

Might it be James Gibson and Deborah Everist, two youngsters from Victoria who had gone missing in 1989? Could one be German tourist Simone Schmidl, unseen since she set off hitchhiking the Hume Highway in January 1991? And what about two other young Germans, Gabor Neugebauer and Anja Habschied, who had disappeared on that same highway on Boxing Day of 1991?

While veterans of the previous investigation such as pathologist Peter Bradhurst got on with the autopsies and the problem of identification, senior police realized they had not just to act quickly but be seen to be doing so. As Gerrard Dutton put it, 'It only really kicked off again when they found the next two bodies, and that's when everything started moving ahead at full speed again.'

Clive Small was then the police local area commander at Liverpool, which lies in the south-western suburbs of Sydney. Now he's the Commander of Crime Agencies for the whole New South Wales police. He remembers getting a call from his region commander: 'He asked me to go down to Belanglo and have a look at the situation there. My thoughts on driving down on the first day were a bit vague, because I didn't know what the situation was, and my purpose was actually to assess it – see whether there was any connection with the bodies that had been found some 12 months earlier, to assess the police response to it, and also to try and work out where the media was going in this matter.'

As he says, 'The only talk of a serial killer at that stage was coming from the media – the police obviously were thinking about it, but weren't talking about it.'

At the latest site, investigators had now discovered a man's black felt hat. Missing Persons said their files suggested it might have belonged to James Gibson. What intrigued the police about that was that they had found Gibson's backpack and camera on the roadside 80 miles north of Belanglo. They later decided that it had been a deliberate attempt by the killer to lay a false trail.

Andy Grosse was busily turning up more crime scene clues, however. A silver chain, a bracelet and a crucifix were found near the smaller skeleton, which seemed to confirm that it was female. And the news that the teeth of the other victim matched the dental chart of James Gibson made it increasingly likely that the woman had been Deborah Everist, as it proved to be as soon as her dental chart had been obtained.

Both victims had been stabbed – but while Gibson had undergone another frenzied knife attack, presumably by a powerful assailant, since Gibson was a fit young man, Everist had not just been stabbed but battered with some blunt instrument.

Clive Small was beginning to reach some conclusions of his own. 'When I arrived, it was clear that several things needed to be looked at. One was the way police were going to conduct this investigation: where were we going from here, and what resources did we need? The second thing was how we were going to handle the media, because they were becoming quite speculative, and that creates the possibility of unnecessary concern in the community, and can also side-track investigations. And another thing was, "How do we stop the fear level increasing in the small local communities?"'

Effectively, Clive Small had already been pencilled in to run a fairly high-profile task force. When he reported back, the response from his superiors was predictable. As he now says, 'I was very lucky to be able to recruit around me the people I wanted, because the service and the Government clearly recognized that this was a very big item, so I basically had a free hand on who I had.'

It was decided at the highest level that this elite squad would be named Task Force Eyre, after Lake Eyre in the centre of Australia. Unfortunately, the police press release announcing this momentous news must have been dictated down the phone – so Task Force Air it was.

When he first heard the news of the fresh discoveries in the forest, Detective Chief Superintendent Rod Lynch was driving in his car with his wife. She asked him if he'd be involved, and he recollects telling her no – 'I just dismissed the matter out of hand: it was a different region.' Then he got the call – Clive Small had a high regard for him, and wanted him as his deputy. 'My role', says Lynch, 'was to remain in Sydney and set up an office. The only area we could locate was very old and dusty: we had to get it clean, we had to find furniture, computers, we had to get renovations done. It was a mess. There was no air-conditioning, and it was coming up Summer – very hot. It was really unfavourable conditions. But it worked out well with the staff I organized – highly motivated people.'

Small also brought in psychiatrist Rod Milton once more. Small knew that with a case like this, 'There was a lot of speculation required – we had victims who were backpackers and therefore isolated from their families and friends who knew them; there was a long time between the murders and the police visitation at the crime scene; a lot of evidence would have been destroyed. And it's that sort of speculation that people like Rod can input.'

Milton's input, as Small recalls, was that 'the offender was probably a loner, probably drove a four-wheel drive vehicle, knew the area well, was very familiar with firearms, was probably a good worker, but in a blue-collar-type job, probably had some sort of stable relationship – he also made the point that he believed he would have come to the notice of the police for some quite serious offences, even though it might have been some time earlier.'

Milton would eventually prove to have justified every minute of police time spent seeking his advice.

Clive Small had no intention of repeating the earlier mistake of suggesting there weren't any more bodies in the forest. A map of the entire area was marked off into grids on the scale of an inch to 750 feet, and teams of 40 policemen were detailed to walk each grid in line abreast. If any of them saw anything of any conceivable interest, they were instructed to halt, shout 'Find' and await a technical specialist who would take photographs, plot the exact position and place anything found in plastic evidence-bags.

Almost a month later, as that fine-tooth comb search

reached the last of the grids and the feeling was beginning to circulate that maybe, after all, no more bodies lay hidden in the bush, a team led by a Sergeant Trichter worked its way into a small clearing. They quickly saw a pair of pink jeans and a length of blue and yellow rope – then an empty carton for .22 bullets. Drink cans with bullet-holes through them. At the very edge, yet again, that curious trademark – a roughly-built fireplace.

It didn't take long for the squad to find the next signature clue: a mound of forest litter with, close by, a bone and a skull. Sticking out from the heap of brush, a boot, with a bone inside.

Gerard Dutton's confident identification of the rifle used in the Clarke murder was still being pursued. The broad sweep approach to Australia's gun dealers having, frankly, done no more than waste police time from Hobart to Darwen, Queensland to Perth, the latest theory was that attention should be focussed on the area surrounding the forest.

While licensed gunsmiths are obliged to keep meticulous records of their sales, nothing prevents a private individual from selling a weapon on to another person without recording or reporting it. And when the police, equipped with a list of those around the forest whose purchase of a Ruger 10-22 was recorded, thought they might impound them for ballistic checks, the scheme was leaked to the media. Which meant, the police assumed, that any guilty owner would promptly dump the gun.

So they turned, perhaps because of Rod Milton's suggestion that the perpetrator would be 'very familiar with firearms', to the local gun club. Their weapons were examined, without any success, but one member did tell investigators that a friend of his had witnessed something rather curious in the area a year or so ago. Police followed up the tip, and talked to his friend.

He told them that he had seen two vehicles, a saloon and an off-roader, driving into the forest. His story was that in the first car he'd seen a driver in front, and between two men in the back was a woman with a cloth tied round her head. In the second were two men, one in front, the other in the back beside another female who also seemed to be bound. Police don't appear to have asked him why he hadn't reported this rather unusual convoy a little earlier, but did ask him to sign his statement.

He signed, 'Alex Milat '.

By now the fifth, sixth and seventh bodies had been identified: Gabor Neugebauer, apparently gagged and strangled as well being shot; Simone Schmidl, who had been stabbed to death, with one powerful blow severing her spinal cord; and Anja Habschied, about whom Peter Bradhurst had even more horrifying news: 'Anja had been decapitated. It was a clean decapitation quite consistent with being done by a sharp instrument, a machete or a ceremonial sword', whereas her companion, Gabor Neugebauer, had been shot six times in the head.

Bradhurst and his colleagues discussed their findings in all seven cases – shootings, stabbings, beatings, and now a ritual beheading – and he is another who now says, 'I tended to favour the view that perhaps more than one person was involved because of the different styles of killing, but I have to say that two types of killing could have been done by the one person if that person was to incapacitate his victims to start with.' A knife blow which cut through the spinal cord would, of course, incapacitate anyone.

The 'two killer' theory was also supported by the heavy log which had been placed over Neugebauer's body. It took three detectives to lift it.

Nevertheless, when Clive Small gave a press conference at which he confirmed the media's long-held opinion that there was a serial killer at large, he used the singular – and, naturally, did not say that his task force was beginning to take a very detailed interest in a whole family in the area which fitted Rod Milton's profile of backswoodsmen with local knowledge, access to four-wheel drive vehicles and a passionate interest in weapons.

Alex Milat had whetted the detectives' interest with his story about the mystery convoy which he didn't report until actually asked about it. One of the many members of the public who crammed the hotlines into Rod Lynch's dedicated office was a woman who said she knew a man who lived near the forest, had lots of guns and a four-wheel drive, called Ivan Milat. And another tip-off concerned a man called Paul Miller who had told workmates there were more bodies to be found before they actually were, and made some very curious remarks about stabbing women: police inquiries established that Paul Miller was, in fact, Richard Milat.

Over the first quarter of 1994, the task force built up a comprehensive dossier on all the Milats – ten brothers, four sisters, born to a Croatian immigrant father and Australian mother – and in particular on Ivan, who turned out to have a very relevant criminal record. He'd collected his first conviction at the age of 17, in 1962, for stealing. Thereafter, he'd added burglary, car theft and armed robbery. And then, in 1971, he'd been charged with rape after picking up two girls who were hitch-hiking along the Hume Highway, driving them off down a track, producing a knife and threatening to kill them if they didn't have sex with him. Very sensibly, one eventually agreed, so long as he didn't use the knife – on which grounds the charge was dismissed, since this was argued to constitute consent.

As Clive Small says, 'Once I'd received the information on Ivan Milat's criminal history, I thought he looked a good suspect, but whether he did or not in a sense didn't matter – it was a matter of whether there was evidence to support it.'

Now the Backpacker Murders had been widely covered in the British papers – and not just because two of the victims were British – over the period from September 1992 to the end of 1993. One reader had followed the story with mounting horror, as the coincidences became too strong to ignore. For when Paul Onions had left the Royal Navy in 1989, he'd decided to backpack around Australia. And on 25 January 1990, he'd checked out of his hostel in Sydney, taken the train to Liverpool and started looking for a ride down the Hume Highway so he could get casual work as a fruit-picker in the south-west.

The ride he'd got was not one he was ever likely to forget.

A silver-coloured four-wheel drive vehicle was outside a shop where Onions called in for a cold drink. The driver, a burly man with a distinctive moustache, asked Paul if he needed a lift and introduced himself as 'Bill.' Onions was later to describe the moustache as being like that of Merv Hughes, a prominent Australian cricketer of the time, but other generations might have called it a Zapata, or even a Frank Zappa. Bill seemed both inquisitive, asking Onions incessant questions about his own background, and forth-coming, revealing to the total stranger in his car that he worked on the roads, came from a Yugoslavian family and lived near Liverpool.

But as the ride went on, somewhere south of Mittagong, Bill's demeanour changed. He began making variations to his speed, and taking repeated glances at his rear-view mirror, and changed from cheerful small-talk to violent abuse of immigrants and 'poms' – of which Paul was clearly one.

Then he suddenly drew to a halt, announcing that he needed to get some tapes from the back of the car. Onions could see a pile of tapes right beside him in the front. Feeling increasingly uneasy, the backpacker also got out of the vehicle – only for 'Bill' to order him back in. He obeyed, but the moment both were back in the front seats 'Bill' pulled out a revolver, pointed it at Paul, told him it was a robbery and then produced a length of rope.

Onions wrenched open the door, and leapt out, leaving his slender backpack behind. As he ran from the car, 'Bill' yelled to him to stop or be shot. Although he was waving desperately at the oncoming traffic to stop, drivers one after another took evasive action, until suddenly Paul felt himself being rugby-tackled from behind. Not long out of the Services, he was fit enough to break free and virtually throw himself in front of the next vehicle. As the driver screeched to a halt Paul tore at the door-handle, leapt in and screamed, 'He's got a gun – help me !'

The driver, Joanne Berry, was herself terrified, at that stage as much of the strange man who had forced his way into her car, in which she and her sister had four children, as of the other man she could see hurrying back to his vehicle, but on balance it seemed best to make a rapid U-turn across the central reservation and drive off as fast as she could. As Paul stammered out his experience, she could tell that he was genuinely in a state of fear, and decided to seek police help.

Mittagong police station was closed, so Joanne carried on into Bowral. There, Paul told his story to Constable Janet Nicholson, giving descriptions of his attacker, the off-road vehicle, of his pack, Sony Walkman and camera, and details of both his British passport and his return ticket back to the UK, which were in his pack. Constable Nicholson put out the descriptions over the radio, although she had no great hopes they'd be productive, and advanced Paul $20 to get back to Sydney, where he reported his losses to the British High Commission, who replaced his passport, if nothing else.

All of which not only stayed with him in the following years, but came sharply to the forefront of his mind as he read the continuing stories of the New South Wales Police pursuing an unknown killer who preyed on backpackers hitching their way southwards on the Hume Highway between Liverpool and Bowral: backpackers who had travelled just a few miles further down the road than he had – because he'd leapt from 'Bill's' car on the verge just before the road enters the Belanglo Forest.

While Paul Onions wondered if the police had kept his complaint on record, Joanne Berry, much closer to the scene in her Canberra home, decided to pick up the phone and call Task Force Air. A detective took note of all she recalled of that frightening afternoon three years before, filed it – and forgot it.

Paul eventually concluded he really ought to do something about his own deep suspicions, and sought advice from his local police back in England. They referred him to the Australian High Commission in London, who gave him the hotline number for the task force in Sydney. On 13 November 1993 he got through to Rod Lynch's chaotically over-worked office and told his story to one of the officers there – who asked him why he hadn't reported the incident at the time, back in 1990. Paul assured him that he had, and was about to give more details when he was instead thanked for his call – and heard the receiver go down.

He rather expected that someone from Sydney would get back to him, but they didn't. For that matter, no one from Sydney brought his call to the attention of the principal investigators.

In fairness, perhaps it should be said that the whole team

was under tremendous pressure, the phones and the computers were close to melt-down and, as Detective Inspector Stuart Wilkins says of his first impressions when he joined the task force, 'From the start it was just chaos – it was bedlam – it was 16 to 18 hours a day. The phones wouldn't stop – there were 12 to 14 phones in the office, and you couldn't move from your desk, because as soon as you hung up from one call the phone would be ringing. Oh, I knew that it would be a very substantial criminal investigation, and I think it's turned out to be the biggest in New South Wales history.'

Wilkins also points out that there were two separate arms to the task force, one in Sydney, one in Bowral, 'and that's two and a half hours apart.'

Even so, it still seems odd how long it took for Paul Onions' statement to travel across the Sydney office. Wilkins remembers that 'it took about three and a half, four months to get to me, and then by the time I worked up the background and did some intelligence work on that information, it was around five months before I got back to Paul Onions.'

The intelligence work presumably included the discovery that Bowral police had lost all record of Onions' original complaint – but fortunately, Constable Nicholson herself was a little better organized, and still had her notebooks from 1990.

Clive Small had more than enough problems on his plate without leads being lost in the bureaucratic jungle. The then-Premier of NSW, possibly because the forest was in his own constituency, had made a highly-publicized visit to the task force and offered a half-million Australian dollar reward for information leading to an arrest and conviction. Small will admit that 'the Premier's appearance upped the pressure.' He had, however, continued to take the view – despite urging from colleagues that they should move in, arrest Ivan Milat and search his property – that 'we needed to do a lot more work before we went that far. We were only going to get one shot at it, and it had to be a good one. I could see us possibly ending up in a situation where we had the prime suspect, we believed we had the offender, but we didn't have the evidence.' Once the news of the calls from Onions and Joanne Berry finally filtered through, the possibility of closing the noose beckoned.

Stuart Wilkins was ordered to ring Paul Onions immediately – in other words, five months after Onions had rung them. 'I contacted him out of the blue from halfway across the world, told him who I was, and what I was doing. You could tell straight away he was apprehensive – in the back of his own mind was the thought, "It might be Milat" or "Is it one of that man's brothers?" so he was concerned, but I established a contact, and made arrangements for him to travel to Australia.'

Given Paul's experiences so far with the New South Wales Police, he can be forgiven for his first reaction when Stuart Wilkins met him at Sydney Airport. 'He asked to look at my badge and my identification', says Wilkins. 'He was obviously scared and apprehensive.'

They booked him into a motel and gave him a day to settle in before asking him to ride down the Hume Highway with accompanying officers and talk them through his experience.

It went well, with Onions recognizing the spot he'd first walked out of Liverpool, and even Lombardy's shop where he'd first encountered 'Bill', but struck a snag a little way south, when their key witness said there had to be a mistake – there should be a small town on the road at this point. The policemen had a moment of panic – until someone remembered that the highway hadn't bypassed it until after 1990.

Onions had no such problems identifying the actual site of his traumatic escape. He took the detectives through his account again, while they noted how close they now were to the forest, and was then driven back to Sydney. His story chimed in exactly with that he had given Constable Nicholson four years earlier – and with that of Joanne Berry. What's more, it had now been established that at the relevant time Ivan Milat had indeed owned a silver off-roader, a Nissan Patrol. He'd since sold it on, but police traced it to its new owner, who had kept something he'd found when cleaning out the car. It was a .22 bullet of the same type as had been used at the Clarke and Waters grave site.

Furthermore, a second interview with Ivan Milat's sister-in-law, the wife of Alex, had finished with her offering the detectives something Ivan had given her. It was a backpack, of a type and manufacture not found in Australia, but made only in Germany. It was Simone Schmidl's.

The day after retracing his journey down the Hume Highway, Paul Onions reported to Sydney police HQ, where he was met by Stuart Wilkins. 'I took him to a video room, and showed him 13 photographs of people who were of very similar description, with the 'Merv Hughes' moustache. After careful consideration and some considerable time, he identi- fied Number Four.'

Number Four was Ivan Milat.

As Wilkins says, 'It was the catalyst that set us off on the operational phase – executing the search warrants which were the final end for Ivan Milat. It was the critical piece of information that solved this case, and it was Paul Onions who did that.'

Clive Small's team had had the premises of all the Milat family under surveillance, both visual and electronic, for some time, but he had deliberately not sent them in to exer- cize the search warrants, which had already been obtained with almost obsessional secrecy, until Paul Onions gave them at least one good holding charge – his identification of a man who had tried to murder him.

Now they could go in. As Small says, 'it was a long day. We had something like 11 different locations, and we didn't know what was going to be found at any of those places. Quite clearly the focus of the arrest was Ivan Milat's place at Eaglevale, and once we did get in, the justification of that focus became quite obvious, because if you were to say all your Christmasses came at once, this was a place where it was like an Aladdin's treasure trove of exhibits.

'The amount of actual incriminating material we found was beyond any of our expectations. The search of Ivan's home, a modest three-bedroom brick house, took three or four days, but the amount of property belonging to the victims –

the amount of property that served to incriminate Ivan – was beyond any of our beliefs. And the interesting part is that it didn't even stop there, because it extended to the homes of other members of the family where further incriminating evidence was found, and in each case, those items had been given to members of the family by Ivan.'

Ballistics expert Gerrard Dutton was one of a four-man search party, also including Andy Grosse, which tackled Ivan's home. 'On the morning of the first day, the most crucial piece of evidence was found. Peter O'Connor was in the ceiling cavity at the time, where the Milats had stored a number of boxes of bits and pieces, including Christmas decorations, which we went through, but Peter was searching every possible nook and cranny, working his way along the wall cavities, lifting up the insulation, shining his torch down – and about a metre down one of them, there was a plastic bag. He looked into it, and then called me over. What was inside that bag were components of a Ruger 10-22 rifle, and of course I recognized them instantly.'

They did not include the barrel – Milat obviously thought that ballistics could only match a bullet to a weapon by the rifling marks. But they did include the breech-bolt, and therefore the firing-pin.

The next day in his laboratory, Dutton test-fired some rounds – and knew that the spent cases he had recovered so many months before had been fired by Milat's rifle.

As the exhibits came flooding in from all the scattered Milat homes, perhaps the biggest shudders were caused by something found in a cupboard in the home of Ivan's mother – a long, curved cavalry sword.

Milat clammed up almost as soon as he was arrested. His line was, and continued to be, that he knew nothing about anything, and that somebody was trying to make him look bad – which, undoubtedly, he did.

He was charged with seven murders. His counsel advised him to plead guilty – and was promptly dismissed for his pains. New counsel were appointed, and immediately began a protracted dispute with the Legal Aid office of the State about their fees.

The actual trial did not begin for another year. It was Australia's biggest-ever murder trial, took nearly three months, heard some 145 prosecution witnesses, examined over 350 exhibits and – despite the defence doing their utmost to suggest that one or more of Ivan's brothers had committed the crimes, and then tried to frame him – the jury took just three days to find him guilty on all seven counts of murder, and the attempted murder of Paul Onions.

He was sentenced to life on each count of murder, and six years for the attack on Onions. The Judge laid down that under no circumstances should he ever be released.

Which leaves two rather uncomfortable thoughts hanging in the air. Did Ivan Milat really act alone? Clive Small will only go so far as to say, 'There's quite strong evidence, I think, that at least some members of the family knew that he was up to no good, and that that no good was pretty nasty – but not to suggest that they knew exactly what it was.'

And might there still be other bodies out there in the bush, perhaps never to be found? Well, police have their strong suspicions in at least four other cases.

But Ivan's brother Boris, interviewed by crime reporters, told them: 'Everywhere he's worked, people have disappeared. If Ivan's done these murders, I reckon he's done a hell of a lot more.'

'How many?' he was asked.

'Oh – 28?' said Boris.